A PHOTOGRAPHIC HISTORY
WORLD WAR I

A PHOTOGRAPHIC HISTORY
WORLD WAR I

R. Hamilton

Photographs by the
Daily Mail

p

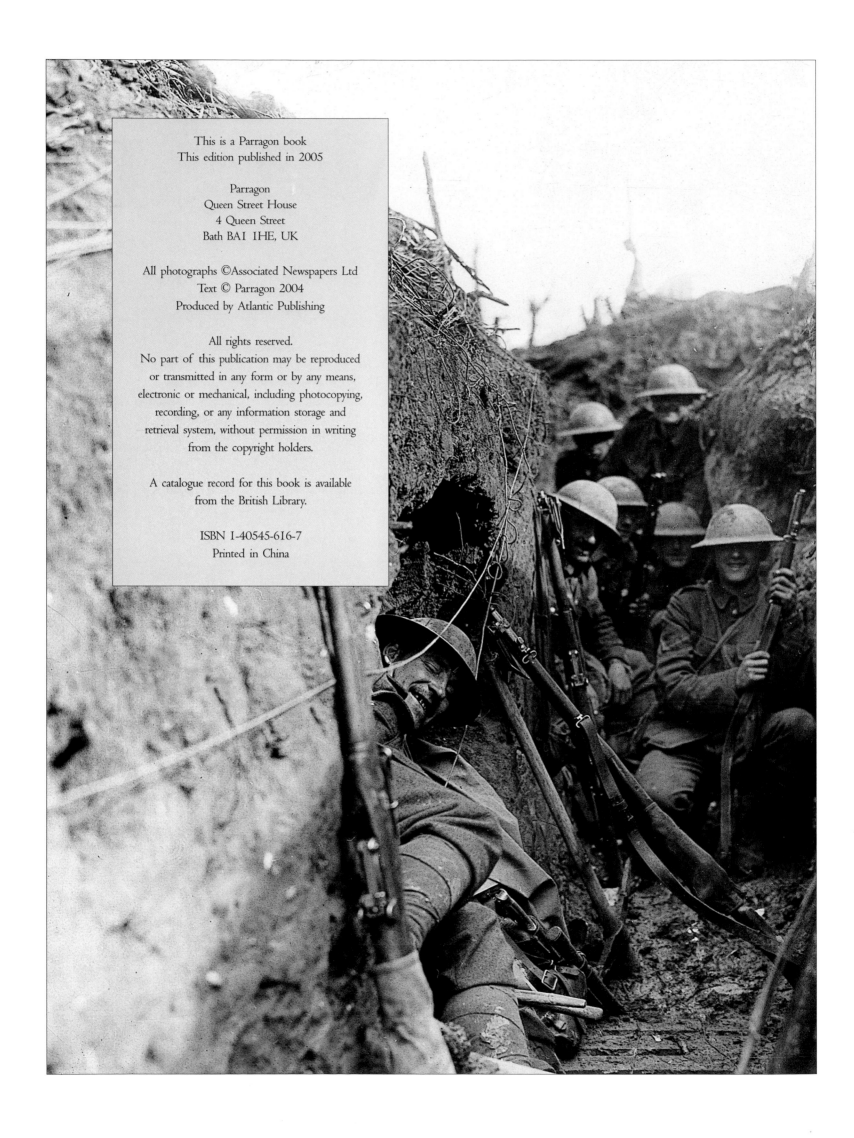

This is a Parragon book
This edition published in 2005

Parragon
Queen Street House
4 Queen Street
Bath BAI IHE, UK

All photographs ©Associated Newspapers Ltd
Text © Parragon 2004
Produced by Atlantic Publishing

All rights reserved.
No part of this publication may be reproduced
or transmitted in any form or by any means,
electronic or mechanical, including photocopying,
recording, or any information storage and
retrieval system, without permission in writing
from the copyright holders.

A catalogue record for this book is available
from the British Library.

ISBN I-40545-616-7
Printed in China

Contents

ACKNOWLEDGEMENTS

The photographs in this book are from the
archives of the Daily Mail.
Particular thanks to Steve Torrington,
Dave Sheppard, Brian Jackson, Alan Pinnock,
Richard Jones and all the staff.

Thanks also to
Maureen Hill, Guy Nettleton,
Cliff Salter, Richard Betts,
Peter Wright and Trevor Bunting.
Design by John Dunne.

The views expressed in this book are those of the
author but they are general views only and readers
are urged to consult a relevant and qualified spe-
cialist for individual advice in particular situations.
Parragon hereby excludes all liability to the extent
permitted by law for any errors or omissions in this
book and for any loss, damage or expense (whether
direct or indirect) suffered by a third party relying
on any information contained in this book.

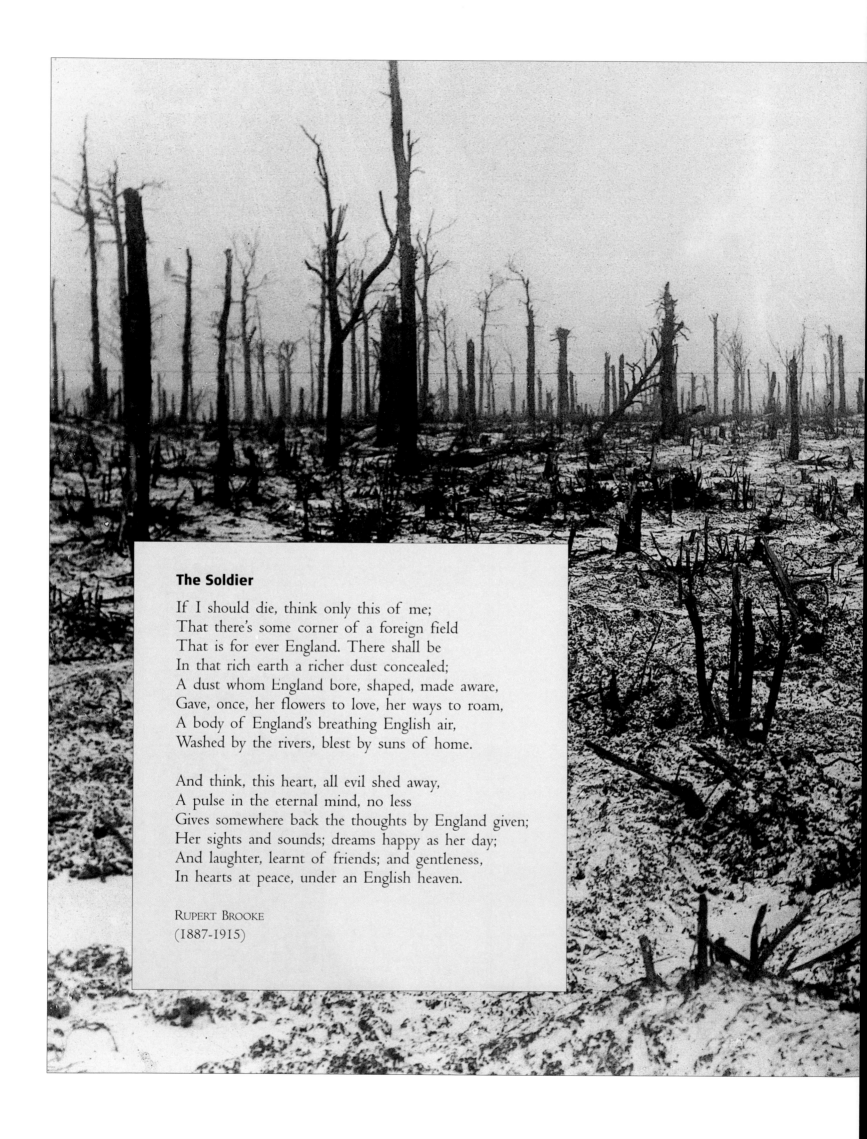

The Soldier

If I should die, think only this of me;
That there's some corner of a foreign field
That is for ever England. There shall be
In that rich earth a richer dust concealed;
A dust whom England bore, shaped, made aware,
Gave, once, her flowers to love, her ways to roam,
A body of England's breathing English air,
Washed by the rivers, blest by suns of home.

And think, this heart, all evil shed away,
A pulse in the eternal mind, no less
Gives somewhere back the thoughts by England given;
Her sights and sounds; dreams happy as her day;
And laughter, learnt of friends; and gentleness,
In hearts at peace, under an English heaven.

RUPERT BROOKE
(1887-1915)

INTRODUCTION

The Great War

By the summer of 1914 Europe was a tinder-box waiting to explode. It was a continent rife with suspicion and resentment, with two power blocs eyeing each other warily. Following the assassination of Archduke Franz Ferdinand in Sarajevo on 28 June, one by one the major powers had taken up arms. The final spark that lit the fuse of war came when Germany invaded Belgium on the morning of 4 August, the day after Britain had affirmed its commitment to defend Belgium's neutrality.

Many welcomed the fact that the waiting was finally over; Europe's nations now had their first opportunity in 40 years to cover themselves in military glory in a good clean, open fight. There was a widely-held conviction that it would all be over by Christmas. Buoyed by public confidence, a fierce sense of patriotism and an eagerness for glory, young men across Europe rushed to join the fighting forces.

The euphoria of those early months soon gave way to the grim reality of attritional warfare in which each side dug into trenches and launched assaults into the no-man's land beween the two. For much of its 52 months' duration the war was a bloody stalemate. Weapon technology had moved on, even since the Boer Wars at the turn of the century, to include aircraft, tanks, flame-throwers and deadly poison gas. Every attack led to massive loss of life. 60,000 died on the first day of the Battle of the Somme alone; more than 10 million lives were lost overall, almost an entire generation of young men.

World War I – A Photographic History examines the causes of the conflict and charts its course on all the major fronts. It describes the collapse of old empires and the birth of new nation states. By the end of hostilities Russia was in Bolshevik hands and the USA had emerged as a global power; the new world order was being established even before the fighting was over.

The 1914-18 conflict did not prove to be 'the war to end all wars'. Faultlines in the peace treaties helped to plunge Europe into an even bloodier war just 21 years later. But it remains a defining moment of the twentieth century. The decisions of the political and military leaders are still being scrutinised and debated, and the consequences of this epic struggle are still being played out.

The narrative is told principally through remarkable photographs, many seen here for the first time, from the *Daily Mail* archive. They are restored to original condition, supported and enhanced by an informative text and enlightening captions. These add to the richness of the photographic detail which captures a portrait of a war fought with great heroism and sacrifice.

This official photograph of a warm, dry, well-fed, smiling Tommy Atkins at the front created an impression far removed from reality. Spirits were high, initially, however, when it was thought the war would be over in a matter of months.

CHAPTER ONE

A Divided Europe

Europe in 1914 was a continent of dynasties and power blocs. With the Ottoman Empire in terminal decline, there were five major players on the European stage: Great Britain, Russia, Austria-Hungary, Germany and France. George V, the second son of Edward VII, acceded to the British throne in 1910, continuing the Hanoverian line which dated back to 1714. Tsar Nicholas II, of the Romanov dynasty, ruled over the vast Russian Empire, as he had since 1894. The Habsburg Emperor Franz Josef I had presided over the Dual Monarchy of Austria-Hungary since 1867. Kaiser Wilhelm II headed the German Empire, having succeeded the Iron Chancellor, Otto von Bismarck, in 1888. Raymond Poincaré, the President of France, led the only republic among the continent's chief power brokers. The First World War would be ignited by an assassin's bullet in Sarajevo on 28 June 1914, but it was the relations between these five powers which held the key. Alliances and enmities that were forged long before that fateful day in the Bosnian capital were the difference between yet another local Balkan difficulty and a worldwide conflagration.

The German Empire was the youngest of Europe's great imperial powers, and its founding sowed the seeds for resentment which would be crystallised in the Great War. The new Reich was formed following a glorious victory in the Franco-Prussian War of 1870-71 when the Prussian Army, backed by Germany, had marched into Paris and exacted a heavy price for peace from the vanquished French: £200 million in reparations and the secession of the provinces Alsace and Lorraine.

France thus had good reason to despise and mistrust her neighbour, and over the next forty years Britain would come to be equally wary. For in that time Germany rapidly developed into a potent industrial and military power. The Kaiser, a neurotic megalomaniac who was invariably photographed in full military regalia, did little to assuage the concerns of countries which feared aggression. Wilhelm cast covetous eyes around him and the chief objects of his envy were Russia and Britain, the latter possessor of an empire on which the sun famously never set. The competitive friction which grew between these nations was not ameliorated by the fact that Kaiser Wilhelm, King George V and Tsar Nicholas II were first cousins. Familial ties would count for nothing when it came to choosing allies and underwriting the security of other sovereign states.

A Powerful Alliance

Suspicion and resentment were rife in the east of the continent, too. Austria-Hungary and Russia were hardly on more cordial terms, and once again the ill-feeling had grown over a number of years. At issue was the fact that Franz Josef's disparate empire included Slavs of the Balkan states, with whom Russia had a natural kinship. Relations between the Austro-Hungarian and Russian Empires had been severely strained since the former's annexation of Bosnia and Herzegovina in October 1908. Russia wasn't prepared to go to war over the issue, however, much to the chagrin of another Balkan country with burning nationalistic ambitions, Serbia. Not only did the Serbs fear that their own land might also be swallowed up by Austria-Hungary, but their hopes for a pan-Slavic state was looking an increasingly distant prospect. Serbia realised it could not take on Franz Josef's mighty empire alone and was forced to accept the status quo. It was a climb-down, one which could only act as a recruiting sergeant for the Black Hand, the secret society committed to the formation of a greater Serbian state. The passion its members held for the cause, and the lengths they were prepared to go to in order to serve it, were encapsulated in the society's motto: 'Unity or Death'. This fanaticism was to be the spark for a continent that was waiting to explode.

The tensions across Europe in the early years of the twentieth century made national security a key issue. Isolation meant possible exposure and vulnerability; dependable allies were needed. Austria-Hungary and Germany had formed an alliance in 1879. They were joined by Italy, whose antipathy to France made that country's decision largely a negative one. Thus was created a powerful central European axis, a state of affairs which exercised the diplomatic minds in London, Paris and St Petersburg. France and Russia had formed a defensive Dual Alliance in 1893, leaving Britain to decide on its position.

'ENTENTE CORDIALE'

At the turn of the century there were those in the British government who favoured an accommodation with the continent's most powerful, and potentially most dangerous, opponent: Germany. Overtures were made but they came to nothing, so Britain turned to France. These traditional enemies had clashed as recently as 1898, almost going to war over a territorial dispute in Sudan. Relations thawed markedly after Edward VII's state visit to Paris in May 1903. It was a triumphant charm offensive, and by the time the monarch left the French crowds were cheering 'notre Roi'. This smoothed the way for the diplomats to get to work, and on 8 April 1904 the two countries signed a historic agreement. The Entente Cordiale, as it came to be known, dealt primarily with outstanding issues between the two in distant corners of the globe. Significantly, it was a friendly understanding, not a formal alliance; neither country was under any obligation to support the other in time of war. But it was a watershed moment in terms of dividing the continent into two rival camps. And three years later, when Britain settled its long-standing differences with Russia, the battle lines were delineated more clearly still. The signing of the Anglo-Russian Convention in August 1907 paved the way for the Triple Entente, a formidable potential threat to the Triple Alliance of Austria-Hungary, Germany and Italy. Crucially, it also

meant that if war did ensue, the countries of the Triple Alliance would have enemies on both eastern and western fronts.

Across Europe many tried to anticipate the flashpoint which would be the precursor to a wider conflict. Some eagerly awaited it. The continent had not seen war for forty years, denying states and individuals the opportunity to cover themselves in military glory, to test might and mettle. Those who felt it would be a relief for the waiting to end almost got their wish in 1911, when France and Germany clashed over their respective interests in Morocco. But although sabres were rattled, the Powers chose peace over escalation. Restraint was also shown in 1912-13, when two Balkan wars were fought. Then, on 28 June 1914, the tinder-box was ignited.

Archduke Franz Ferdinand, the 51-year-old nephew of Franz Josef and heir to the Habsburg throne, was well aware of the potential danger of his visit to Sarajevo. There had been previous assassination attempts by disaffected Bosnian Serbs, and for his well-publicised trip through the streets of the capital that June day he wore a jacket of a specially woven fabric that was thought to be bullet-proof. Franz Ferdinand had a reforming zeal for this part of the Austro-Hungarian Empire. Oppression of the Serb population would end under his leadership, but that was a future prospect; for now his intention was to win over the people - but to take suitable precautions just in case. Ironically, the Archduke's moderation helped to galvanise the Black Hand into action. If oppression had fanned the flames of Serbian nationalism, a more tolerant incumbent of the Austro-Hungarian throne might dampen the ardent desire of those committed to see a Greater Serbia established. From the moment the Archduke's visit to Sarajevo had been announced, the Black Hand had got to work in earnest.

ASSASSINATION IN SARAJEVO

In the event, the seven-strong assassination squad had fortune on their side. After a failed attempt to blow up the car carrying the Archduke and his consort Sophie, it seemed that the gang had lost their chance. But as one of their number, 19-year-old Gavrilo Princip, was pondering his next move, he was confronted by his target. The driver of the Archduke's car had taken a wrong turn, and Princip turned his 22-calibre Browning pistol on its occupants. Franz Ferdinand was struck in the neck; Sophie, who was pregnant with their fourth child, took a bullet to the stomach. Both were soon declared dead.

Austria-Hungary immediately decided that the trail of guilt led to Belgrade and determined to exact a high price from Serbia over the events in Sarajevo. The Habsburg Empire was outraged by the murders, but it wanted more than mere revenge; this was a perfect pretext to teach Serbia a lesson. If the Serbs were crushed and humbled, it would consolidate an empire that was in danger of becoming fractured.

With Russia, long-standing friend of the Serbs, waiting in the wings, Austria-Hungary sought assurances from its chief ally, Germany. The bellicose, unstable Kaiser sanctioned any action that Franz Josef's government saw fit to take against Serbia. He couldn't risk Austria-Hungary falling to a two-pronged attack, from Serbia in the south and Russia in the east. Moreover, Wilhelm may have calculated that if a European war was imminent, then it might as well be fought at a time of Germany's choosing. And Germany was ready now.

On 23 July the Austrian government issued an ultimatum to Serbia. Its very specific demands and the imposition of a forty-eight-hour time limit for a reply prompted Britain's Foreign Secretary, Sir Edward Grey, to remark that, if Serbia accepted, it would be 'the greatest humiliation I have ever seen a country undergo'. Yield Serbia did, but not to the letter of the demand, not to the point of threatening its very existence as an autonomous independent state. Austria-Hungary was spoiling for a fight; on 28 July war on Serbia was formally declared.

Russia initially tried to steer a narrow course, caught between a desire to support her Serb brothers whilst not antagonising Germany. Partial mobilisation - against Austria-Hungary alone was considered, but this proved unworkable. On 31 July Germany issued Russia with an ultimatum of its own: to cease mobilisation forthwith. No reply came and the following day Germany declared war on its eastern neighbour.

THE MARCH TO WAR

A mere forty-eight hours would elapse before Germany was also at war with Russia's ally, France. The Reich was far from idle during that period, however, for time was of the essence. Germany had long feared the prospect of war on both her eastern and western fronts and had contingency measures for just such an eventuality. The Schlieffen Plan, as it was called, involved a rapid strike to neutralise the threat from France, after which German forces could turn their full attention to Russia. Speed of action was critical to the plan's success. The full might of the German Army had to be in position on the eastern front before Russia was ready to fight. The geography of the latter country meant that there was a window of opportunity before it posed a threat to Germany. But it was a window which would be soon be slammed shut. Accordingly, even before war was formally declared between Germany and France, on 3 August, German forces were on the march westwards.

Under the Schlieffen Plan, Germany aimed to attack France through Belgium, rather than directly across the border which the two countries shared. Not only was Belgium a neutral country, but both Germany and Great Britain were long-standing guarantors of that neutrality. The Kaiser was obviously quite prepared to disregard this commitment when faced with a greater prize. But what would Britain's stance be?

Many powerful voices in Asquith's government were vehemently against Britain becoming sucked into a European conflict. Thorny domestic issues, notably the question of Home Rule for Ireland, provided a difficult enough agenda, and Britain was under no treaty obligation to take up arms. On 3 August the Belgian government rejected German demands to be allowed unhindered passage through their country. Albert, King of the Belgians, looked to Britain - and so did Germany. To the amazement of the German Chancellor, Theobald Bethmann-Hollweg, the Asquith government unequivocally chose to honour its commitment to Belgium. Germany's efforts to persuade Britain to stand aside while Belgium and France were invaded had come to nothing. The French were having grave doubts as to whether the Entente Cordiale would bring Britain to their aid; but in the event it was the violation of Belgium which dissolved almost all remaining opposition to war amongst the British Cabinet.

On 4 August it was Britain's turn to deliver an ultimatum, expiring at midnight that day. If German forces did not withdraw from Belgium, Britain would declare war. The deadline came and went. An incredulous Bethmann-Hollweg remarked: 'Just for a scrap of paper Great Britain was going to make war on a kindred nation who desired nothing better than to be friends with her.' If Germany had badly misjudged Britain, Sir Edward Grey was far more perceptive. While there was widespread euphoria among the peoples of all the belligerents in August 1914, Grey was in sombre mood: 'The lamps are going out all over Europe; we shall not see them lit again in our lifetime.'

OUTBREAK OF WAR

The rival powers each anticipated a short, successful war. Bullish German troops posed next to road signs which read 'To Paris'; equally bullish French troops did the same next to signs indicating the way to Berlin. This was hugely optimistic, if not flawed, thinking. Even if one of the protagonists succeeded in landing a heavy pre-emptive blow, it was never likely to result in capitulation. The reason was simple: this was a war of alliances. If, for example, France suffered grievously from a German onslaught under the Schlieffen Plan, she was hardly likely to yield as long as Britain and Russia stood by her side. And although Italy stood on the sidelines, refusing to take up arms with her Triple Alliance partners, Germany and Austria-Hungary also gained strength from the knowledge that they all stood together. In other words, the same alliances that had been triggered, domino-style, to bring Europe to war also militated against a quick victory for either side.

Even so, the Central Powers, as the German and Austro-Hungarian forces were known, received early encouragement. German forces swept through Belgium and the fortress town of Liège fell, a strategic victory that was vital to the success of the Schlieffen Plan. On 17 August the Belgian government removed from Brussels to Antwerp; three days later the capital was also in German hands. Reports of atrocities emerged, and it soon became clear that the German Army wanted more than mere subjugation; it intended to obliterate anything in its path and crush the spirit as well as succeed militarily. The sacking of the cathedral town of Louvain in the last days of August shocked the civilised world. The magnificent university library, with its many priceless books and manuscripts, was destroyed. The invading force claimed that shots had been fired against the army of the Reich, and many civilians paid the ultimate price. A month later Rheims Cathedral suffered a terrible bombardment, despite the fact that a Red Cross flag flew from its tower.

The French, meanwhile, were putting their own plan into action. Led by Field-Marshal Joseph Joffre, French forces concentrated their efforts on an offensive through Lorraine, hoping to make inroads into German territory thereafter.

Although aware of the broad principles of the Schlieffen Plan, the French calculated that the Germans would overstretch themselves in attacking through the Low Countries, leaving a soft underbelly on the Franco-German border. It wasn't soft enough. The German army, swelled by the use of reservists, easily repulsed France's attack. From strong wooded positions, German machine guns cut down in droves French soldiers who had insisted on joining battle in brightly-coloured tunics to show their style. Joffre soon had to rethink his strategy. If his men couldn't achieve a breakthrough, then the Germans must be prevented from doing so. Joffre duly redeployed large numbers to the west, where British forces were also now gathering.

BRITAIN ENTERS THE BATTLEFIELD

The British Expeditionary Force, consisting of some 50,000 troops and five cavalry brigades, crossed the Channel and was soon in the thick of the action. Led by Sir John French, the BEF met German forces at Mons in the last week of August. Although heavily outnumbered, the regular British troops were a match for an army that included many reservists. At the same time, the French Fifth Army, under General Lanzerac, faced the German onslaught at nearby Charleroi. The Germans were not forced back in these battles but at least a brake was applied to their progress.

The Schlieffen Plan now started to unravel. The vast German front was supposed to pivot south and then push eastwards, taking in Paris before closing in on the main French contingent on the Franco-German border. But the German generals were struggling to reinforce the huge front their men were fighting on, and were further hampered by the fact that Belgian forces had blown up many key communication routes. The German line was being stretched too thinly and was manned by troops who were exhausted and under-resourced. The response was to close ranks, but this had adverse consequences. It meant that when the German right wing, under General von Kluck, swung south, the army was west of Paris; instead of sweeping through the capital, it now lay behind them, untouched.

Failing to march into Paris was a military as well

as a psychological blow, for it meant that von Kluck's army was itself exposed, liable to attack from the rear. Joffre saw his chance and knew it was time to strike. Von Kluck was forced to turn west to face the threat of the French Sixth Army. During the Battle of the Marne, which began on 5 September, von Kluck's westward surge meant that his men had become dangerously isolated from the nearest German contingent, Field Marshal von Bulow's Second Army, which was now some 30 miles away. Fearing that this gap would be exploited by the Allies, the Germans opted for a tactical retreat. They withdrew to a strong position on high ground north of the River Aisne, with Allied forces in pursuit. Neither side could make further headway.

STALEMATE ON BOTH FRONTS

As it was proving impossible for either side to breach the enemy line, both spread out laterally instead, a manoeuvre that was dubbed the 'Race to the Sea'. There was just one serious attempt to break the deadlock in this time, the month-long First Battle of Ypres. On 31 October the Germans held the initiative after breaking through at Gheluvelt, on the Menin-Ypres road. The Allies rallied but at great cost, particularly to the BEF, which was all but wiped out. The status quo was restored, and as winter set in the opposing armies dug in along a line which eventually stretched from the North sea to Switzerland. All thoughts of a swift victory evaporated; it was now a war of attrition.

There was stalemate, too, on the Eastern Front. With their forces concentrated in the west, the Germans were content with a short-term holding operation against the Russian army. The Austro-Hungarian forces, with their multi-ethnic make-up and indifferent leadership, were nowhere near as formidable as those of the Reich. Russia thus took the initiative, two of her armies gaining a foothold in East Prussia in mid-August. Germany was forced to retreat. This reverse prompted the recall to active service of retired Field Marshal Paul von Hindenburg, with Erich von Ludendorff transferred from the Western Front as his Chief-of-staff. Together, these two would become the most important figures in Germany's strategic planning. They were also soon national heroes.

Hindenburg and Ludendorff stopped the Russian advance in its tracks. The full might of the German Eighth Army was first turned upon General Samsonov's forces in the south. The Russians were routed in the Battle of Tannenberg and Samsonov took his own life. Hindenburg now turned his attention to the Russian First Army, gaining yet another comprehensive victory over General Rennenkampf's forces on 9-10 September. East Prussia was back in German hands.

GERMANY'S ALLIES

The lustre of Hindenburg's triumph for the Central Powers was tarnished by events further south. The Austro-Hungarian forces, which had invaded Serbia in the first days of the war, had their early gains snatched away from them. The aged King Peter, determined to lead from the front, galvanized the dispirited Serbs and near-defeat was turned into a stunning victory. By mid-December a largely peasant army had driven the Austro-Hungarian army back across the Danube.

Germany's ally fared little better against the Russians, suffering a heavy defeat at the Battle of Lemberg. Such reverses would prompt one German general to remark that being bound to Austria-Hungary was like being 'shackled to a corpse'. Even so, as 1914 drew to a close the knockout blow proved as elusive in the east as it had in the west. Neither side had the manpower or tactical supremacy to gain a decisive edge; neither side was so weak or tactically inept to invite failure.

The balance was tilted somewhat when Turkey joined the fray in early November. The Turks sided with the Central Powers, hoping to arrest the decline of the Ottoman Empire by joining forces with the winning side. Russia's Black Sea coast came under attack, and Britain, France and Russia all declared war on a new foe. Although it gave the Allies yet another front on which to fight, Turkey's intervention was still not of an order which would tip the balance in favour of a swift victory. By the end of the year — by which time the conflict was supposed to be over — early optimism gave way to the grim reality of a long, drawn-out struggle.

Britain Declares War

5 August 1914: The following
announcement was issued at the Foreign
Office at 12.15am:-
'Owing to the summary rejection by the
German Government of the request made
by His Majesty's Government for assurances
that the neutrality of Belgium would be
respected, His Majesty's Ambassador in
Berlin has received his passports, and His
Majesty's Government has declared to the
German Government that a state of war
exists between Great Britain and Germany
as from 11pm on August 4.'

Above: Europe's nations now had their first
opportunity in forty years to cover themselves
in military glory. There was a widely-held
conviction that it would all be over by
Christmas. Buoyed by public confidence,
young men across Europe rushed to join the
fighting forces. Here Lance-Corporal C A
Jarvis (second right), who became the first
British soldier of the war to be awarded the
Victoria Cross, is pictured at Woodford
Green recruiting station, using his celebrity to
encourage civilians to enlist.

Above: Lance-Corporal E Dwyer, another recipient of the VC, gives a rallying speech before a large crowd in Trafalgar Square.

The Angel of Mons

By 22 August 1914 a 120,000-strong British Expeditionary Force had reached French soil, an operation that had taken just two weeks to complete. The very next day Field Marshal Sir John French's men were called into action. They met the German army at Mons, where it quickly became apparent that they and the French forces were in danger of being enveloped and overwhelmed. A retreat was ordered. The exhausted men of the BEF spoke of seeing a spectral figure in the sky brandishing a sword and keeping the German army at bay. The legend of the Angel of Mons was born.

The Schlieffen Plan

Field Marshal Alfred von Schlieffen devised a plan to avoid waging war on both eastern and western fronts. He believed that Russia's military machine would be slow to mobilise and that a knockout blow could be delivered against France before the threat in the east became serious. The plan involved a powerful wheeling manoeuvre through Holland and Belgium, sweeping south to engulf Paris. Schlieffen died in 1913. His successor, General Moltke, put a watered-down Schlieffen Plan into effect when war broke out. He weakened the army which swept through the low countries by choosing to reinforce the border with Germany - the exact opposite of what Schlieffen recommended. Moltke further undermined the plan by redeploying troops to the Eastern Front when news came through that the Russian army was making inroads into East Prussia. The chance of a decisive quick victory over France was lost and Germany had to contend with its worst fear: war in both east and west.

Above: 'Kitchener's Army' on the march. Between the outbreak of war and the introduction of conscription in 1916, some 2,500,000 men volunteered for active service.

Left: Britain's decision to maintain only a small professional army created huge problems. When men enlisted in droves there wasn't enough equipment to go round, or personnel to train them. Broomsticks often replaced rifles during exercises.

Below: A group of children accompanies some new recruits. As the casualty figures escalated so age and height restrictions for recruits were increasingly relaxed.

Schlieffen Plan begins to unravel

By late August 1914 the British and French armies were on the back foot. German forces had made sweeping gains through Belgium but they too were in trouble. The ambitiousness of the Germany's Schlieffen Plan meant that its soldiers were overstretched, under-supplied and exhausted. Instead of encircling Paris from the east, in accordance with the original plan, German forces lay to the west of the capital. Events on the Eastern Front further undermined Germany's position in the west when German commander General Moltke redeployed two corps to shore up the 8th Army in its fight against the advancing Russians. It was a fatal error. The replacements could not have arrived in time to influence the outcome of the Battle of Tannenberg; the decision simply deprived the German army in the west of resources it could ill afford to lose at so critical a juncture.

Above: Fallen soldiers at the Battle of the Marne, September 1914. The German army withdrew to take up defensive positions on higher ground at Aisne.

Battle of the Marne

With Paris under threat of being overrun, the Allies chose this moment to strike back. The fact that the enemy lay to the east of the capital afforded a golden opportunity; it was the weakened German army that was now exposed and at the Battle of the Marne, fought between 5 September and 10 September, the Allies forced the Germans to retreat. The Schlieffen Plan lay in ruins. A shattered Moltke soon paid the price of failure. Within days Erich von Falkenhayn succeeded him as supreme commander of the German army.

Above: Wounded soldiers arriving at Ostend, having failed to prevent the fall of Antwerp on 9 October 1914. The Western Front now stretched from Switzerland to the North Sea.

War brings new role for women

The First World War was a watershed for women. The recruitment of Kitchener's Army left labour shortages, and these were even more acute after the introduction of conscription in 1916. Before the war it was mainly single women who were in paid employment, and their chief occupation was domestic service. The conflict gave them the opportunity to move into jobs which were more skilled or better paid and often both. The fact that this also supported the war effort made this new economic role even more attractive to women. The Suffragette movement was quick to demand that women should have a 'right to serve', although this naturally had political overtones. A step towards equality was made in July 1918, when married women over 30 were finally granted the vote.

Opposite: Women workers helping to solve the munitions crisis of 1915.

The Eastern Front

In accordance with the Schlieffen Plan, Germany allocated minimal forces on the Eastern Front in an effort to win a quick victory in the west. When war broke out General Prittwitz's 8th Army was charged with this holding role. He faced two Russian armies, led by General Rennenkampf and General Samsonov, who advanced into East Prussia. The Russian troops were poorly trained and led, but sheer weight of numbers presented Germany with a huge threat. Prittwitz panicked and ordered a retreat, a decision which led to his being replaced by von Hindenburg and Ludendorff.

Above: Russian troops presented a threat to East Prussia sooner than Germany had anticipated.

Right: The remnants of the Russian 1st and 2nd armies in full-scale retreat after the crushing defeat by von Hindenburg at the Battle of Tannenberg.

Battle of Tannenberg

The Russian armies split into two to
bypass the Masurian Lakes, after which
they planned to combine in a pincer
movement on the German army. The
Germans intercepted radio messages and
knew of this plan. As his army was at a
numerical disadvantage, von Hindenburg
settled on a plan to meet the Russians
before they joined forces. The German
8th Army swiftly moved south to meet
Samsonov's men, scoring a decisive victory
at Tannenberg on 27 August 1914.
30,000 were killed, almost 100,000 taken
prisoner. Samsonov took his own life.

Above: Men of the
new Royal Naval
Division, holding
defensive positions in
Antwerp on the
Western Front as the
city is evacuated.

Above: The British fleet, viewed from the deck of HMS *Audacious*. It was widely believed that Britain still reigned supreme on the seas, although more than a century had passed since Trafalgar. At the beginning of the war most of the Navy's larger ships were stationed at Scapa Flow or Rosyth in Scotland with smaller ships grouped around the British coast.

Opposite: The Grand Fleet, pictured shortly before war was declared. It would be almost two years before Admiral Sir John Jellicoe was able to test his ships against the German navy in the one significant maritime battle of the war at Jutland.

Russian defeat buys time for France

After victory at Tannenberg, von Hindenburg turned his attention to Rennenkampf's army. Battle was joined on 9 September and the outcome was the same, although Rennenkampf did prevent a complete rout by ordering a retreat. A triumphant Germany acclaimed von Hindenburg and Ludendorff. For Russia there was one crumb of comfort: in defeat she had relieved the pressure on France by forcing a hasty redeployment of German forces from west to east. Time was critical to the success of the Schlieffen Plan. Even in defeat Russia had helped to ensure that Germany did not meet its aim of victory on the Western Front in six weeks.

Above: British troops in Belgium, whose invasion had finally decided the Asquith government to declare war. Britain had been a guarantor of Belgian neutrality since 1839.

War in the air

By 1914 there was widespread interest in aviation for its many civilian applications. Military leaders were generally sceptical about the use of aircraft as a tool of war. Volume was one problem. The number of airworthy planes the combatants had between them amounted to just a few hundred and they were prone to mechanical failure. Finding pilots to fly them was another issue. During the course of the war training would be reduced to just a few hours before men took to the skies. The high attrition rate didn't help matters.

Above: British marines on the march in Ostend. Germany's advance through Belgium was punctuated by a series of atrocities. Execution and rape were used as part of a deliberate policy of *schrecklichkeit* – frightfulness.

Above: British sappers at work. The men responsible for engineering, construction and demolition work made a crucial contribution to the war effort.

Life in the trenches

On 13 October 1914 the *Daily Mail* printed the account of a visit to the newly-dug trenches:

'Our men have made themselves fairly comfortable in the trenches, in the numerous quarries cut out of the hill-sides, and in the picturesque villages whose steep streets and red-tiled roofs climb the slopes and peep out amid the green and russet of the woods. In the firing line the men sleep and obtain shelter in the dug-outs they have hollowed or 'under-cut' in the sides of the trenches. These refuges are slightly raised above the bottom of the trench, so as to remain dry in wet weather. The floor of the trench is also sloped for purposes of drainage. Some trenches are provided with head cover, the latter, of course, giving protection from the weather as well as from shrapnel balls and splinters of shell.'

Left: British troops disembark in France shortly after war was declared.

Below: Royal Scots Fusiliers dug in during the winter of 1914. As Germany was entrenched on enemy soil the onus fell on the Entente Powers to find a way of removing them. Almost all military leaders at the time believed that offensives would bring reward, albeit possibly at great cost. World War I showed that the costs were invariably high, the rewards modest.

Above: Lord Kitchener (left), hero of the campaign to win back the Sudan in 1898, was appointed Secretary of War by prime minister Asquith and charged with recruiting a large army to fight Germany.

Left: Allied troops in France. The German army came tantalisingly close to taking Paris in August 1914. Many fled the capital, fearing that its fall was imminent.

Below: The scale of the casualties meant there was a need for places where the wounded could receive treatment. 'Hospital huts' were fabricated in England and shipped across the Channel.

Above: The geography of the Eastern front meant that the war in that theatre didn't become entrenched. The battles fought in the east were more akin to those that might have occurred in a 19th-century conflict.

Opposite: Even when not under attack soldiers had much to endure in the trenches, which often flooded. Trench foot, a form of frostbite, was common.

Christmas truce

Although hostilities were of a scale and ferocity hitherto unseen, the battlefield did bring fellowship. This even extended to the enemy; the combatants recognized that no side had a monopoly when it came to duty and honour and that all would have liked nothing better than to go home to their families. On Christmas Eve 1914, in sub-zero conditions, this camaraderie manifested itself in good-humoured banter and well-wishing across no-man's-land. Competitive carol-singing briefly replaced the desire to gain territory and kill. Makeshift altars were constructed to celebrate Mass and for once soldiers had no fear of sniper fire. The commanding officers on both sides were unimpressed by this impromptu display of humanity and compassion and the truce was inevitably short-lived.

Lord Kitchener, Secretary of State for War.

CHAPTER TWO

Germany Takes Territory

On Christmas Day 1914 the opposing forces in the advanced western trenches put their enmity in abeyance and exchanged pleasantries in no-man's land. It was but a temporary respite. The new year brought fresh initiatives to try and break the impasse. Perhaps technology held the key. Aircraft, tanks, flame-throwers and poison gas would all be deployed, but these were still in their infancy; there remained the widespread belief that victory would go to the side which possessed the mightier battering ram of men and shells.

By the end of 1914 some German commanders felt that, with the failure of the Schlieffen Plan, Germany could not secure victory. One of the Entente powers would have to be removed from the equation. General Erich von Falkenhayn, Germany's new Chief-of-Staff, favoured a fresh onslaught on the Western Front. The British Expeditionary Force had been wiped out and Britain was replacing them with volunteers rather than conscripts. It would be some time before 'Kitchener's Army' was ready for battle, and Falkenhayn realised this was a window of opportunity. However, Austria-Hungary needed reinforcing, and if the Central Powers wanted to pick off one of her enemies, Russia was the natural target. A huge redeployment of troops from west to east thus took place. Russia had done well enough against the ramshackle forces of Germany's ally; how would she fare against the awesome military machine of the Reich itself?

RUSSIANS IN RETREAT
The territorial gains in the east were some of the most spectacular of the entire conflict. At the start of the

year the Russians held a line some nine hundred miles long, stretching from the Carpathians to the East Prussian Frontier. Yet, they would soon be in full-scale retreat. Lemberg and Przemysl, such recent glorious triumphs for the Russian army, were both reclaimed by the Central Powers in June. The Allies were stunned but not surprised when Warsaw fell on 4 August. The only crumb of comfort in London and Paris was to applaud a well-executed tactical retreat. Reviewing the first year of the conflict on 15 September 1915, War Secretary Lord Kitchener told the House of Lords:

'The success of this great rearguard action has been rendered possible by the really splendid fighting qualities of the Russian soldier, who in every case where actual conflict has taken place has shown himself infinitely superior to his adversary. It is these fighting qualities of the men of the Russian Army which have empowered her able generals and competent staff to carry out the immensely difficult operation of retirement of a whole line over some hundred to two hundred miles, without allowing the enemy to break through at any point or by surrounding their forces, to bring about the tactical position which might involve the surrender of a considerable portion of the Russian Army.'

This was a charitable view based on political expediency rather than military reality. The truth was that the ill-equipped Russian forces were in disarray, and their ability to live to fight another day had more to do with Falkenhayn's reluctance to press home his advantage than any shrewd manoeuvring on the part of the retreating ranks. Tsar Nicholas certainly saw little merit in his army's performance. He sacked his Commander-in-Chief, Grand Duke Nicholas, and took personal control of his forces in the field. More significant perhaps, was that, although the Russians were on the back foot, they were not cowed into submission. German hopes for an early armistice in the east were dashed.

HEAVY CASUALTIES

On the Western Front it was a year of heavy casualties for little gain. While Kitchener's recruits were undergoing a rapid programme of military training, the Allied trenches in France and Belgium were largely manned by the French. The National Register Bill, introduced in July 1915, required every man and woman between the ages of 15 and 65 to submit personal details, but the question of undertaking national service remained a polite enquiry; Britain would hold out against conscription for another year.

Below: 1915 would see a new weapon deployed on the battlefield: deadly poison gas.

Opposite: Soldiers on leave, pictured at Waterloo Station. For many, returning to Blighty would be an unfulfilled dream.

Germany's redeployment of eight divisions to the Eastern Front meant a significant weakening of the Reich's forces in the Western theatre. But Germany had a new weapon to compensate for the lack of manpower. Gas was first used by the Central Powers in the east at the beginning of the year and by April Britain and France also had to contend with this new threat, described by Sir John French as 'a cynical and barbarous disregard of the well-known usages of civilized war and a flagrant defiance of the Hague Convention.'

It was on 22 April, the start of the Second Battle of Ypres, that the western Allies were first confronted with a thick yellow asphyxiating gas cloud. There was chaos in the Allied line, but the Germans were naturally wary of following up too quickly and exposing themselves to the chlorine's deadly effects. Using makeshift respirators of handkerchiefs soaked in water or urine, the Allies rallied. By the end of the battle, on 13 May, the stalemate remained.

The Allies, meanwhile, planned offensives of their own. On 10 March they made their first serious attempt to break the enemy line, at Neuve Chapelle. The village was successfully wrested from German hands, although Sir John French's report made grim reading: 12,000 men either killed, wounded or missing for a gain of three hundred yards on a front of half a mile.

The Battle of Neuve Chapelle and the Second Battle of Ypres exposed a dire shortage in Britain's munitions production. Demand far outstripped supply and when this reached the public domain it precipitated a political crisis. In May the Liberal

government was replaced by a coalition. Asquith retained the premiership, while Lloyd George was moved from Chancellor of the Exchequer to a new department, the Ministry of Munitions.

AERIAL BOMBARDMENT

The war was also being waged at sea and in the air. Zeppelins had bombed Paris in the early days of the conflict, and on 19 January 1915 British civilians had to face an aerial bombardment for the first time. Parts of the Norfolk coastline were the first to come under attack, with further raids on the south-east and North Sea coast in the following months. Fatalities were few but the fact that they were almost all non-combatants added a new dimension to the conflict. It was called 'frightfulness' at the time; terror tactics in modern parlance. This new strategy on the part of the Central Powers was more about damaging morale than inflicting huge casualties. It was a policy that was also soon in evidence on the high seas.

On 18 February 1915 Germany declared the waters around Great Britain and Ireland a war region. This did not mean that the German fleet had to emerge from the safety of Kiel in order to prosecute the war. Instead, using submarines and mines, Germany blockaded the waters around the British Isles. The Allies were employing a similar tactic, putting to good use the fact that control of the North Sea provided a natural blockade of the German fleet. Both sides were wary, the Allies of the U-boat threat, and the Germans of committing themselves to a sea battle against the superior numbers of the British fleet. This shadow-boxing could bring no quick reward. And the perceived inactivity of the mighty Royal Navy earned it scornful comments from many in the trenches. The Germans tried to increase the effectiveness of their blockade by announcing that commercial shipping would be attacked without warning. Winston Churchill, First Lord of the Admiralty, speaking in the House of Commons, condemned Germany's new terror threat as 'open piracy and murder on the high seas'.

On 7 May the Cunard liner *Lusitania* was sunk a few miles off the Irish coast with the loss of over 1000 lives. The German embassy in Washington had issued a statement a week earlier announcing that the vessel was a potential target but few took the threat seriously enough to cancel their trip. The US government responded to the loss of 128 American lives only with strong words, but the sinking of the *Lusitania* generated powerful anti-German feelings across the Atlantic and would be the first step along the way to the USA's entry into the war. These same feelings would also be widespread in Britain, where animosity often spilled over into violence. Shops with German connections, real or imagined, were attacked by angry mobs. Prince Louis of Battenberg had already resigned as First Sea Lord, faced with prejudice against his Germanic origins. The same sentiments would lead the royal family to adopt the name of Windsor.

GALLIPOLI

When war broke out the Allies' naval strength had been regarded as a vital factor in the forthcoming struggle. The first six months had shown little evidence of that supremacy, but in early 1915 an Anglo-French task force was deployed in the Mediterranean with the aim of changing all that. The plan was to attack Turkey through the Dardanelles, the narrow waterway

from the open sea which led all the way to Constantinople. If that city could be taken there was every chance of forcing a passage through to their Russian allies, a major strategic coup.

In February the forts at the entrance to the Straits were bombarded by a fleet led by Vice-Admiral Sackville Carden. Progress up the Straits was slow and on 18 March three battleships were lost to mines. It was decided that the success of the campaign depended on the deployment of land forces. On 25 April British and French troops, together with soldiers from the Australia and New Zealand Army Corps, landed on the Gallipoli Peninsula. Everything was against Sir Ian Hamilton's men: the weather was bad, the terrain difficult and the enemy forces strongly positioned. John Masefield, the future Poet Laureate, commanded a hospital boat off Gallipoli and offered this insight to those who wished to picture the scene:

'Imagine the hills entrenched, the landing mined, the beaches tangled with barbed wire, ranged by howitzers and swept by machine guns, and themselves three thousand miles from home, going out before dawn, with rifles, packs and water bottles, to pass the mines under shell-fire, cut through the wire under machine-gun fire, clamber up the hills under fire of all arms, by the glare of shell bursts, in the withering and crashing tumult of modern war, and then to dig themselves in in a waterless and burning hill while a more numerous enemy charges them with the bayonet.

'And let them imagine themselves enduring this night after night, day after day, without rest or solace, nor respite from the peril of death, seeing their friends killed and their position imperilled, getting their food, their munitions, even their drink from the jaws of death, and their breath from the taint of death. Let them imagine themselves driven mad by heat and toil and thirst by day, shaken by frost at midnight, weakened by disease and broken by pestilence, yet rising on the word with a shout and going forward to die in exultation in a cause foredoomed and almost hopeless.'

Hopeless it proved. With the Allies pinned down, a fresh landing at Suvla was carried out in August but this was quickly nullified. By November it was clear that retreat was the only option. Churchill, one of the chief advocates of the campaign, had spoken of being just 'a few miles from victory', but those few miles remained a far-distant prospect. Sir Charles Munro replaced Hamilton, and he was charged with leading the evacuation. Churchill resigned. The withdrawal at least was a spectacular success. It was effected between December 1915 and January the following year with barely a casualty, although the

Below: Rifles were standard issue for infantrymen, but on the battlefields of World War One the machine gun proved its deadly worth. The German Maxim and British Lewis guns accounted for countless lives during the conflict.

entire campaign had cost the Allies more than 250,000 men. Turkey's success in preventing the Allies from gaining access to the Black Sea and linking up with the Russian Army was that country's most significant contribution to the Central Powers' war effort.

HAIG TAKES COMMAND

The autumn of 1915 saw Joffre planning yet another offensive on the Western Front. Driving the enemy from French soil was the over-arching concern in spite of the harsh experience of the spring offensive. Joffre clung to the hope that throwing yet more manpower and weaponry at the German line might bring the desired outcome. It didn't. British troops, however, fared better in the advance in Artois and Champagne. Sir Douglas Haig's First Army took Loos, and this time it was the German soldiers who had to contend with a gas attack, the first time that British forces had used this instrument of war. Lack of reserves prevented the attack from bearing fruit and the German forces were able to rally. Sir John French was blamed for keeping the reserves too far from the action, an error of judgment which would see him replaced by Haig as Commander-in-Chief of the British Expeditionary Force in December.

As the year drew to a close the Central Powers were in the ascendancy. Britain suffered a major blow

in Mesopotamia, where her interests had become vulnerable targets since Turkey's entry into the war. In September a force led by General Charles Townshend took Kut-el-Amara but an attempt to push on to Baghdad proved to be a hopeless undertaking. As with Gallipoli, a bold offensive turned into full-scale retreat. Townshend's exhausted men struggled back to Kut. Though they held out for 143 days on paltry rations – just a little flour and horsemeat by the end – the outcome was inevitable. The surrender would finally come in April 1916, with some 13,000 men taken prisoner by the Turks.

THE GERMAN ADVANCE

By the year's end the great German advance in the east had yielded remarkable territorial gains: Ukraine, Lithuania, modern-day Poland and parts of Belarus. Nor were they finished yet. In the autumn Austro-Hungarian forces mounted yet another assault on Serbia, this time with German support. For the Serbs it meant another attack from the north-west, but now the country faced a further difficulty, from the east. Bulgaria threw in her lot with the Central Powers in October. Ferdinand, Bulgaria's ruler, had been seduced by offers of parts of Serbian land, a bribe which played well with a country that had been forced to cede territory to Serbia during the Balkan wars. The addition of Bulgaria's weight to the attack on Serbia was crucial. When Anglo-French forces tried to help their Balkan ally by entering the country via Greece, Bulgarian troops blocked their way. Serbia was on her own.

Belgrade was quickly overrun and the Serbs were forced into a full-scale evacuation of the country, through the harsh mountain regions of Montenegro and Albania. Thousands perished on the flight to the Adriatic coast, from where the survivors were taken to Corfu in Allied ships.

Despite the considerable successes the Central Powers enjoyed in 1915 they had not achieved their great aim: to force one of the Entente Powers to the negotiating table. And by now the Allies had been bolstered by the addition of Italy to their ranks, the former Triple Alliance member switching sides in May 1915. The new year would bring a fresh attempt to break the deadlock: the long-awaited major sea battle between the naval superpowers, Britain and Germany.

Above: A fortunate wounded soldier is helped to safety by a comrade. The exigencies of war meant that the injured often lay dying on the battlefield. Soldiers spoke of being haunted by the agonised cries of the fallen in no-man's land.

Churchill targets Gallipoli

As stalemate set in on the Western Front the Allies looked to strike at the enemy elsewhere. Winston Churchill, First Lord of the Admiralty, championed the idea of an Anglo-French naval assault on Turkey via the Dardanelles, a narrow 35-mile strait which opened out into the Sea of Marmara. From there Constantinople was within sight. This in turn was a gateway to the Black Sea, and a successful operation would allow British and French forces to establish a vital communication link with their Russian allies.

Above: British troops on a landing exercise. At the beginning of 1915 the British Army was preparing to attack the Dardanelles.

Left: Allied leaders in discussion during the Gallipoli campaign. Kitchener was among those who initially favoured the plan, only to change his mind in the light of heavy losses. Winston Churchill, First Lord of the Admiralty, remained wedded to the Gallipoli campaign throughout.

Left: The Battle of Neuve-Chapelle, on the Western Front, was launched by Haig on 10 March 1915. The first major British offensive resulted in the village of Neuve-Chapelle being taken. There were some 25,000 casualties at the end of the three-day battle, divided evenly between the combatants.

Below: A naval assault on the Dardanelles was attempted in February-March 1915 but failed, making a land campaign necessary. The chief problem for the Allies was the mobile batteries operated by Turkish forces. These were wreaking havoc and could easily be resited, preventing Allied guns from destroying them. Troops on the ground were needed for that.

A British Officer's Account of a Visit to Victims of Gassing

'Their faces, arms, and hands were of a shiny grey-black colour, with mouths open and bead-glazed eyes, all swaying slightly backwards and forwards trying to get breath. It was the most appalling sight, all these poor black faces, struggling, struggling for life, what with the groaning and noise of the efforts for breath. There is practically nothing to be done for them except to give them salt and water to try to make them sick. The effect the gas has is to fill the lungs with a watery, frothy matter which gradually increases and rises till it fills up the whole lungs and comes up to the mouth; then they die. It is suffocation; slow drowning taking in some cases one or two days.'

Daily Mail, 7 May 1915

Above: The Belgian town of Loos was devastated by the battle there, launched 25 September 1915. It was here that the British deployed poison gas for the first time. Adverse wind conditions resulted in the gas being blown back towards the British lines in places.

Above: British soldiers returning from
front-line duty at the Battle of Loos.
Sir John French was criticised for his
handling of reserves in the attack, and
in December 1915 he was replaced as
Commander-in-Chief of the British
Expeditionary Force by Haig.

Above: November 1915. Troops trying to keep warm as they face the prospect of a second winter at war.

Below: British soldiers on their way to the front. The conviction remained that throwing increasing numbers of men into the fray would bring the desired victory. This view would persist through 1916 and 1917.

Right: Troops on the
Eastern Front are
wrapped up to keep out
the cold.

Below: Surgeons worked in
emergency theatres behind
the front line. However,
despite medical advances,
many men died of
infections which could
not be easily treated
before the development
of antibiotics.

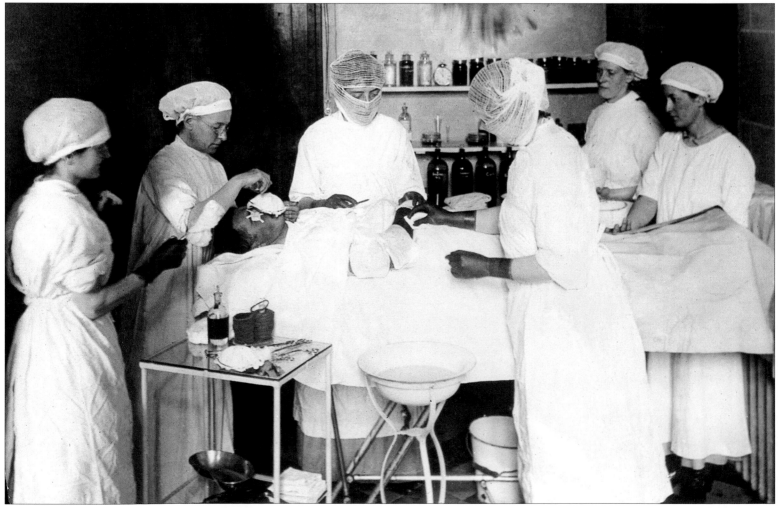

Poor omens for Gallipoli campaign

The Gallipoli landings began on 25 April 1915. The operation was led by Sir Ian Hamilton, although he remained aboard the *Queen Elizabeth*. Communications was just one problem facing the invading army. They knew little about the strength of the enemy. In fact, during the weeks of the abortive naval attack the Turks had considerably strengthened their forces. The Allies had taken most of their knowledge of the terrain from tourist guides. It did not augur well for the success of the campaign.

Above: Soldiers survey the battlefield. Head wounds were common in the trenches and each army produced protective helmets intended to reduce the number of injuries. British soldiers wore a bowl-shaped helmet made of steel designed by John L. Brodie in August 1915.

Above: A vigilant British soldier keeps
watch. The trenches constructed by the
German army were generally considerably
deeper - up to 40 ft. in places - and far
more elaborate.

Left: War separated families and loved ones. For the mothers, wives and sweethearts left behind there was the dread of receiving a telegram beginning with the words: 'It is my painful duty to inform you…'

Below: The 1915 FA Cup Final was a subdued affair, held in Manchester on a damp afternoon before a crowd of only 50,000, many of whom were servicemen displaying signs of the injuries sustained in battle.

Britain Experiences its First Aerial Attack

The first Zeppelin raid on Britain took place on the night of 19 January 1915. Yarmouth was the target. This was the first of 51 raids, mostly on the east coast and London, which resulted in 557 fatalities. Many of these were women and children; total war meant that civilians too faced the prospect of paying the ultimate price. As new fighter and bomber planes appeared so the number of Zeppelin raids decreased. Weaponry was developed to strike at these large, slow and highly inflammable craft. By 1918 they were virtually redundant.

Above: Letters and parcels from home provide a welcome fillip for soldiers at the front. This was also a war of propaganda, however; the images that were made available were carefully controlled.

Left: Sorting the mail which carried festive greetings from home, Christmas 1915.

Below: Canadian troops enjoy a break from duty, if not mud. As an imperial power Britain was able to draw on manpower from all corners of the globe. The *Daily Mail* greeted their arrival in Plymouth in October 1914 with the following words: 'For all that Canada has done in this war, for her splendid troops, for her gifts, for her instinctive comprehension of the stake that is on the table, and above all for the spirit in which she has asserted her right to take a hand in the game, the British people are profoundly grateful. Never was the assistance she has so lavishly offered more welcome and never was it more needed.'

Troop rotation

Trenches were constructed in lines. All commanders recognised that rotation was necessary and that there was a limit on how long a man could tolerate being in the front line. As soldiers were moved back to the reserve trenches the pressure eased somewhat and allowed men to recover, mentally if not from any physical ailment.

Left: A Scottish infantryman tries out a new type of headgear, with support straps to help carry loads that could be anything up to 60lb.

Opposite: Three styles of British uniform: officer's garb on the left, private's on the right, while a member of a Scottish regiment sports the kilted version.

Above and Left: A light-hearted moment as soldiers optimistically suggest that the wreckage of a Hansom cab might make it to the seat of government. Morale was a vital issue. There would be large-scale insurrection by disaffected troops on both sides, and many executions were carried out during the course of the war.

Opposite: When they were not partaking of mud-tainted meals, Canadian troops spent some of their off-duty moments playing baseball.

Right: The senior military strategists continued to put their faith in fresh offensives to break the deadlock on the Western Front. The experience of Gallipoli reinforced the idea that attritional warfare would yield a breakthrough in France and Belgium.

Below: Germany and its allies made spectacular gains on the Eastern Front in 1915 taking Przemysl, Lemberg and Warsaw. The Second Battle of Ypres, which was fought between 22 April and 25 May 1915, was the Germans' only offensive on the Western Front that year.

Above: In May 1915 the British
and French were buoyed by
Italy's decision to join the
Entente Powers, despite having
been a member of the Triple
Alliance.

Right: Fixing bayonets for a fresh offensive. In 1915 the Allies repeatedly tried to make the decisive breakthrough, launching attacks at Aubers Ridge, Vimy Ridge and Artois. Joffre was preoccupied with removing the enemy from French soil and clung to the belief that continued attacks with élan would bring success.

'They went down like corn in front of a scythe'

An excerpt from the letter of a young Lieutenant in the Northamptonshire Regiment printed in the *Daily Mail* gives a vivid picture of life in the trenches:

'We have the satisfaction of knowing that if we suffer, they suffer very, very much worse. The * * * took 800 prisoners yesterday, and the 48th took fifty more this morning. Several of them speak English, and they say they haven't had any food for four days. Others are such youngsters - some of them only seventeen to nineteen years old. Last night they charged us three times. They came on about five deep (the Germans always keep close formation). We let them come up to about fifty yards of our trenches, then let 'em have it for all we were worth with rifles and machine-guns. They went down like corn in front of a scythe. It was glorious and yet awful. We then finished 'em up on the bayonet.'

Above: Troops aboard SS *Nile*, preparing to land on the Gallipoli peninsula.

Opposite: The Anglo-French fleet used in the Gallipoli campaign consisted mostly of outdated battleships. The exception was the super-dreadnought *Queen Elizabeth*, whose 15-inch guns it had been hoped would destroy the Turkish defences and make a land campaign unnecessary.

Heavy Anzac casualties at Gallipoli

The Gallipoli campaign got off to the worst possible start when the Anzacs disembarked at the wrong point. As they tried to scale some difficult inclines they suffered grievous casualties. Elsewhere many did not even reach dry land and the water ran red. Those who successfully established a beachhead found themselves trapped between the sea and the hills. It took only a modest number of Turkish soldiers with machine guns on high ground to derail the Allies' plan almost before it got under way.

Above: Anzac troops on their way to Gallipoli. The huge losses they suffered at 'Anzac Cove' would go down in history as a testament to their bravery and sacrifice.

Above: Suvla Bay, September 1915. The Allies had landed reinforcements here the previous month in the hope of averting a disaster. They too quickly became bogged down in entrenched warfare. The *Daily Mail* reported 'The attack from Suvla was not developed quickly enough, and, as recounted in the War Office communiqué of the 19th inst., was brought to a standstill after an advance of about 20 miles.'

Monro advises withdrawal from Gallipoli

Spring turned into a baking summer in the
Dardanelles. The combination of broiling heat and
corpse-strewn beaches brought disease, which
accounted for many more Allied lives. Far from being
the lightning raid that was envisaged, the Gallipoli
campaign turned into yet another entrenched battle,
the very thing the military leaders had sought to avoid.
In August the Allies tried to break the deadlock by
landing reinforcements at Suvla Bay. It made no
difference and in the autumn General Sir Charles
Monro, Hamilton's replacement, advised evacuation.

Above: In May 1915
a truce was declared
at Gallipoli for both
sides to bury their
dead. The summer
brought many more
casualties and in the
autumn the wisdom
of the campaign was
finally questioned.

Left: In the summer of 1915 Allied troops had to contend with searing heat, which brought a widespread outbreak of dysentery, a further impediment to any hope of success.

Below: Marines on guard duty during the ill-fated Gallipoli campaign. The inhospitable terrain was a key factor in its ultimate failure.

Left: The Dardanelles campaign was conceived as an alternative to the stalemate that had set in on the Western Front. In fact it too became synonymous with deadlock and heavy losses. Churchill, one of the chief proponents of the campaign, resigned when the decision to withdraw was taken.

Above: After putting up with the intense summer sun many soldiers fell victim to frostbite as temperatures plummeted in the autumn. General Sir Charles Monro finally took the decision to end the Gallipoli campaign and plans were laid for a mass evacuation.

Opposite: A member of the Australian Imperial Guards organises musical entertainment while keeping watch for Turkish soldiers, who were barely 30 yards away.

Gallipoli successfully evacuated

The evacuation from Gallipoli at least was a complete success. The Allied withdrawal took place in late December 1915 and early January 1916. Not a single life was lost as many ingenious tricks were employed to fool the Turkish army into thinking the Allied positions were still occupied. Even so, casualties for the whole campaign were a quarter of a million.

A wounded soldier receives a welcome helping hand. The events of 1916 would lead many front-line troops to question the cause they were fighting for, though the camaraderie remained unshakeable.

CHAPTER THREE

A Deepening Stalemate

Despite the reverses of 1915 the Allies went into the new year with renewed optimism. Kitchener's recruits would soon be ready for battle and the munitions crisis had largely been overcome. But the question of turning these advantages into military success remained. The Central Powers were adept at redeploying from one battle zone to another as the need arose, and the Allies now determined to implement an obvious counter-measure. At a meeting at Chantilly in December 1915 it was decided that new offensives on the main fronts had to be better co-ordinated. Concerted attacks would stretch the enemy's forces, hopefully to breaking point.

Germany's plan for the new year also involved a major fresh assault in the west. 1915 had seen the Central Powers assume mastery of the Eastern Front and Falkenhayn now proposed to repeat the trick in France. He was astute enough to realise that France and Britain could not be overrun, nor did they need to be. Falkenhayn believed that there were strategic targets in France, well within reach of his army, that would bring the desired outcome. If one of these could be taken, or merely threatened, the patriotism and pride of the French would demand nothing less than total commitment – even total sacrifice – to prevent what in cold, detached terms would be a modest territorial loss. The historic city of Verdun, situated on the River Meuse, was identified as the place where the French would willingly bleed to death. And when that happened, Falkenhayn concluded, Britain too would be mortally wounded. The Reich's troops received a seductive exhortation: that their efforts in the forthcoming struggle at Verdun would result in peace being signed in that city. With such high stakes it was little wonder that the siege of Verdun was called Operation Gericht (Judgment).

THE BATTLE OF VERDUN

The Germans stole a march by launching their offensive first. The Battle of Verdun began on 21 February 1916. Twelve hundred guns, including the famous 42-centimetre Big Bertha, launched one of the fiercest bombardments of the entire war. In previous battles artillery was the precursor to an infantry advance; at Verdun Falkenhayn envisioned a huge bombardment concentrated on a mere eight-mile front as the key to victory.

On the fourth day the Germans took Fort Douaumont, the largest of the city's famous defensive strongholds. As predicted, the French refused to cede a city that was a symbol of national pride, regardless of the fact that it was of no great strategic value. The German trap was sprung. But the French were not content merely to become cannon fodder to a hopeless cause. Under General Pétain, who assumed command of the city's defences, they would fight fire with fire.

Pétain was a general of the modern school, recognising that noble sacrifice with élan – the traditional French way – had at times to become subservient to technology. His own artillery began inflicting heavy casualties on the German ranks. With lines of communication badly damaged, Pétain also made sure that one key road to the south of the city remained open. The 'Voie Sacrée' or 'Sacred Way', as it became known, would be remembered for the ceaseless

snake of trucks carrying fresh troops and supplies to
the front, bringing exhausted and shell-shocked men in
the opposite direction for well-deserved rest and
recuperation. Pétain, the man who would be reviled as
a collaborator in World War II, became a national hero
for the part he played in helping to save Verdun.

The battle raged until June. Unsurprisingly, there
was by now some wavering among the Reich's hierarchy.
A victory that was expected within days had failed to
materialise after four months. With a decision on
Verdun in the balance, news came through of a major
Russian offensive in the east. General Alexei Brusilov's
rout of the Austro-Hungarian army forced Falkenhayn
into a large-scale redeployment to that theatre. No
sooner was this done than British forces began their
own offensive on the River Somme. Falkenhayn had
missed his chance and the action at Verdun was scaled
down. During the remainder of the year the French
regained all the territory they had lost. The aggregate
death toll was about 700,000, with French losses
marginally the greater. Yet again it was carnage on a
monumental scale for no discernible benefit. Even so,
President Poincaré proudly declared Verdun an 'inviolate
citadel' defended by men who had 'sowed and watered
with their blood the crop which rises today'. The
Verdun campaign cost Falkenhayn his job, and he was
replaced as Chief-of-Staff by Hindenburg in August.

SOMME OFFENSIVE

France played a supporting role as the Allies now
launched their own offensive on the Somme. A huge
week-long artillery bombardment was a prelude to an
attack by front-line troops on 1 July. As with the
German army in February, optimism was great among
Allied troops who sang: 'We beat 'em on the Marne,
we beat 'em on the Aisne, we gave them hell at Neuve
Chapelle and here we are again'. However, the artillery
attack had not done its work, proving ineffectual against
the heavily entrenched enemy. Worse, it gave the Germans
prior warning of the imminent assault. The infantry
attacked in close ranks and were easy prey for the
German Maxim machine guns. By nightfall the casualty
figure stood at 57,000, the worst day in British military
history. The more tactically astute French made some
gains but overall it was a black day for the Allies.

Haig was undeterred by the losses. Although
never as bad again, the overall verdict of the Somme
offensive made grim reading. Positions Haig had hoped

to secure on the first day were still in German hands
in mid-November. Allied casualties exceeded 600,000,
with German losses up to half a million. The
campaign had seen British tanks deployed for the first
time, but these did not make the impact that had been
hoped for. By the end of the year a decisive
breakthrough on the Western Front remained as elusive
as ever.

1916 saw the death of the man whose
recruitment campaign had seen more than two million
British men enlist since the outbreak of hostilities.
Lord Kitchener was aboard HMS *Hampshire* bound for
Russia when the ship was sunk off the Orkneys.
Despite his efforts the rate at which men were
volunteering had slowed by the start of 1916. The
Government responded by introducing the Military
Service Bill on 5 January. Single men aged 18-41
would now be conscripted. Asquith wanted the sons of
widows to be exempted, but this quickly fell by the
wayside. The exigencies of war – and the huge losses
on the Western Front in particular – meant that before
the year was out married men up to the age of 41
were also being called up.

In addition to Britain's new conscripts, the
Allied ranks were swelled in August 1916 by a new ally,
Romania. It was hoped that King Ferdinand's decision
to join the Entente Powers might tip the balance in
their favour in the Balkans, but that quickly proved to
be wide of the mark. 'The moment has come to liberate
our brothers in Transylvania from the Hungarian yoke,'
said the King, but on 5 December Bucharest fell almost
without a struggle. If recruiting; allies or conscripts
made no tangible difference in 1916, what of the
long-awaited battle for supremacy on the high seas?

THE NAVAL BATTLE

For nearly two years the British and German fleets had
avoided full-scale confrontation. Despite the furious
efforts of the Reich leading up to war it was the
British navy which had more ships and greater
firepower. The mighty Dreadnought, whose turbine
engines could propel it to 21 knots and whose 12 inch
guns had a ten-mile range, was a formidable fighting
machine. However, the first Dreadnought had appeared
in 1906 and Germany had had a decade in which to
respond in kind. Moreover, the Royal Navy hadn't been
tested in battle since the days of Nelson and was led
by Admiral Sir John Jellicoe, a cautious man who had

grown up in the age of steam.

Wary of German mines and torpedoes, the British fleet had been executing a distant blockade policy. Based at Scapa Flow, Jellicoe's ships had a natural stranglehold on the North Sea and the German fleet remained tied up in harbour for long periods. In January 1916 the new commander of Germany's High Seas Fleet, Admiral Reinhard Scheer, masterminded a plan to neutralise Britain's naval superiority. Scheer knew that to prevent his country from being slowly starved of resources, he had to attack. His plan was to split up the enemy fleet, thus increasing his chances of victory. Raids on Britain's east coast were carried out, forcing Jellicoe to deploy a battle-cruiser squadron south to Rosyth. Phase one of Scheer's scheme had been accomplished. Phase two was to lure the battle cruisers into the open sea by parading a few of his own ships off the Norwegian coast. The battle-cruiser squadron, led by Sir David Beatty, duly obliged. Lying in wait not far from the German outriders was the entire High Seas Fleet. Unbeknown to Scheer, however, British intelligence had cracked the German naval code. Scheer had hoped to overpower the battle-cruiser squadron and escape before the main British fleet could reach the scene. But, thanks to the code-breakers Jellicoe was already steaming into action.

THE BATTLE OF JUTLAND

Beatty's squadron engaged the enemy at around 4pm on 31 May 1916. He was soon faced with two major reverses as both the *Indefatigable* and *Queen Mary* exploded and sank within twenty minutes of each other. Only two of *Indefatigable's* 1,019-strong crew survived, and 1,286 men lost their lives on the *Queen Mary*. A bewildered Beatty famously commented: 'There seems to be something wrong with our bloody ships today.' Later investigation would suggest that the way in which the cordite was stored was the Achilles heel of a powerful fighting machine.

Not only was German gunnery having the better of the exchange but Scheer was closing in fast. When Beatty sighted the main body of the German Fleet he turned his battle-cruisers north towards Jellicoe and the Grand Fleet. It was now Britain's turn to try and lure the enemy into a trap.

When the battle lines were drawn it was Jellicoe who held a huge tactical advantage. By the time the two fleets engaged his ships were arranged broadside across the German line, a manoeuvre known as 'crossing the T'. The German fleet came under heavy bombardment and, despite the loss of the *Invincible* in yet another spectacular explosion, Jellicoe seemed assured of success. Scheer's answer was to effect a brilliant 180-degree turn, his ships disappearing into the smoke and confusion. Jellicoe, ever mindful of exposing himself to torpedo fire, was reluctant to follow, but soon discovered

Below: The combination of shell craters and heavy rain produced difficult terrain, both for men, animals and motor vehicles, including the latest battlefield weapon: the tank.

that he didn't need to. For inexplicably, Scheer's forces performed a second about-face manoeuvre and headed directly back towards the British line. Jellicoe was in a dilemma: to engage carried the prize of an outright victory, but with German torpedoes now within range there was a considerable risk of further losses. He chose discretion and retreated. By the next morning the German fleet had slipped away. The Battle of Jutland – or Skagerrak, as the Germans called it – was over.

Germany hailed it as a great victory, and with some justification since Britain's losses were substantially higher. Fourteen ships of the Grand Fleet had been sunk, while Scheer had lost eleven vessels. Over 6,000 British sailors lost their lives; Germany's casualties were less than half that number. There was certainly disappointment in Britain both at governmental level and in the population at large. On the other hand, Germany never threatened Britain's mastery of the seas again. Scheer advised the Kaiser that maritime strategy should now focus on the deployment of U-boats, not surface ships.

Below: Millions of pounds of explosives were used on some of the battlefields of the Western Front, resulting in a completely desolate landscape.

Opposite: Water or urine-soaked handkerchiefs were first used to counter the threat of poison gas. Respirators were soon developed and the threat was largely nullified.

A PROTRACTED CONFLICT

Both on land and at sea, 1916 had been as indecisive as its predecessor. By the end of the year each of the protagonists faced a new threat: destabilisation from within. War weariness set in. The privations of a protracted conflict meant that the euphoria of August 1914 was now a distant memory. Each country sought to quell unrest within its own borders while actively encouraging it within those of its enemies. Britain's greatest crisis came at Easter, when Sinn Fein members took over Dublin's Post Office. The uprising was brutally put down and the rebel leaders were executed. Meanwhile in the Middle East Britain was actively trying to foment revolution in pursuance of its war aims. The Arabs of the Hijaz were moved to rise up against the Ottoman Empire on British promises of post-conflict independence. T. E. Lawrence, who played a prominent part in the guerrilla war that the Arabs began to wage, knew from the start that Britain had no intention of honouring its pledge. The seeds of mutiny and revolution were sown in 1916; the following year would witness a dramatic harvest of these pent-up feelings which would affect the course of the war.

With the strain showing and disaffection growing, the desire for a settlement naturally gathered momentum. On 12 December 1916 Germany sued for peace. But the note that was passed to the Allies spoke of the 'indestructible strength' of the Central Powers and stated that 'a continuation of the war cannot break their resisting power'. Unsurprisingly, such language was hardly seen as magnanimous among the Entente Powers. Lloyd George, who had replaced Asquith as prime minister in December 1916, gave a trenchant reply. It was a 'sham proposal' and entering into discussions on the basis of its contents 'would be putting our heads in the noose with the rope end in the hands of the Germans'. All sides may have been eager to end hostilities, but not at any price.

Right: Spoils of war:
one infantryman
sports a German
greatcoat while
another has attached
an eagle emblem to
his helmet.

Below: Evacuating
Suvla Bay in the
Dardanelles. The
Allies employed many
tricks to cover the
evacuation of
Gallipoli. These
included Heath
Robinson-like
contraptions which
would fire weapons,
giving the impression
that positions were
still manned.

Falkenhayn targets Verdun

At the beginning of 1915 Germany's commander Erich von Falkenhayn targeted France as the weaker of the Entente Powers of the Western Front. He believed that the French were already at their limit of endurance and devised a plan which would bring the country to its knees. Falkenhayn surmised — correctly — that by attacking Verdun, a city of historic significance, France would defend it to the last drop of blood. Verdun was of negligible strategic value; indeed, without it the French line would have been shortened, bringing a welcome saving in resources. But practical considerations were of secondary importance: Verdun was a symbol of national pride and had to be defended at all costs.

Above: French *poilus* manning the trenches. At the beginning of 1916 Falkenhayn hoped to repeat the success the German army had enjoyed against Russia during the previous year.

Right: By the beginning of 1916 the rate at which volunteers were enlisting had slowed. The British government responded by following the example of every other major combatant and introducing conscription.

Below: Canadian troops being inspected and greeted by General Sam Hughes, April 1916. Britain's Empire contributed considerable numbers of troops to the Allies fighting force. Australia sent more than 400,000 soldiers to fight in Europe, and 59,000 of these did not return. Canadian forces lost some 60,000 men in the conflict and India almost as many. Sixteen thousand New Zealanders died, many of these at Gallipoli.

'Judgment' day for Verdun

The attack on Verdun, codename 'Operation Gericht' – Judgment – was launched 21 February 1916. Falkenhayn's plan to crush the French at the historic French town began with a massive artillery bombardment concentrated on a narrow 8-mile front. Over 1,200 guns were used, including the famous 42cm Big Bertha – named after the stout wife of Gustav Krupp, in whose factory it was made. The French, who had only belatedly appreciated the full extent of the threat, suffered heavy losses. Within four days German troops had taken Fort Douaumont, the largest of the city's fortresses, with barely a shot fired.

Above: The French town of Armentieres was taken by the British in October 1914. Until it was captured by the German army in April 1918 it served as an important forward base for the Allies.

Left: Two Salvation Army women offer support and comfort to troops billeted in France. Nurses apart, women were a rare sight in forward positions.

Above: On the home front, Women took on all manner of jobs traditionally done by men, though rarely did they achieve equal pay. The Trades Union movement was generally hostile to the new role women played in industry and commerce.

Pétain, defender of Verdun

Field Marshal Joffre charged General Henri Philippe Pétain with the task of defending Verdun. Unlike most French military leaders, Pétain recognised the value of artillery in paving the way for infantry attacks. Under his leadership the French began to strike back. Beyond the narrow front which the Germans had opened up, the French were able to regroup. Pétain saw that a clear line of communication was vital to keep the front well supplied and to put his policy of troop rotation into practice. To this end he made sure that the 'Voie Sacrée', the single secure route, was kept open. For seven months this road would see unbroken lines of two-way traffic 24 hours a day.

Above: Secretary of State for War, Lord Kitchener (right), pictured with a former incumbent of that post, Lord Haldane. Kitchener's influence in the Cabinet had declined by the end of 1915, although he remained a popular figure with the public.

Left: French soldiers had precious little rest in 1916. For ten months they fought and died in the defence of Verdun, exactly as Falkenhayn had predicted.

Verdun offensive stalls

By May 1916 the German offensive at
Verdun began to stall, although on 7 June
Fort Vaux was taken. This came only
after an heroic effort by the 600-strong
garrison who were reduced to drinking
their own urine before they were finally
forced to surrender. Such deeds ensured
that Verdun would forever be associated
with the iron will of the French in
defending their land.

Above: French front-line troops,
pictured May 1916. Three months
into the Battle of Verdun the
German army was continuing to
make gains, including Mort
Homme, the aptly named 'Dead
Man'. Falkenhayn closed down the
offensive on 11 July to release
troops for the Somme.

Allies plan Somme offensive

In December 1915, the month in which Haig replaced Sir John French as Commander-in-Chief of British forces, the Allies met to discuss battle plans for the new year. It was decided that a large-scale Anglo-French offensive around the River Somme would be mounted. The German onslaught at Verdun, launched in February 1916, forced the Allies to alter their thinking. Crucially, French troops were redeployed en masse to staunch the haemorrhage at Verdun; only five of the original 40 divisions were left at the Somme, which thus became largely a British offensive.

Above: Russian soldiers on training exercises in France, May 1916.

Left: Fort Douaumont, the largest of Verdun's famous fortresses, fell to the Germans on 25 February 1916.

Right: On 31 May 1916 the
British and German fleets – the
two greatest naval forces in the
world – finally joined battle off
the coast of Jutland. The battle
was indecisive. German ships
inflicted heavier losses, but then
withdrew and did not risk a
second engagement for the
duration of the war.

'The greatest naval battle of the
war was fought off the Danish
coast on Wednesday, with the
result that the British Navy has
to mourn heavy losses. But
according to the late Admiralty
report this morning, the enemy's
losses were practically as heavy.
Three battle-cruisers (nearly one-
third of our total battle-cruiser
force at the opening of the war)
have been sunk, and a number of
other ships are sunk or missing.
We lament our dead; we know
them to have fallen gloriously;
and they have done their best.'

Daily Mail, 3 June 1916

Right: Northumberland
Fusiliers go over the
top at La Boiselle on
the first day of the
battle of the Somme.
This village was an
important strategic
target and fell to the
allies on 6 July, 1916

Relief for Verdun

By the spring of 1916 the French were desperate for the Somme attack to begin in order to divert German resources and provide relief for beleaguered Verdun. They finally got their wish on 24 June, when a week-long bombardment was launched. Unlike Falkenhayn, who was more interested in 'bleeding the French white' at Verdun than in making territorial gain, Haig believed that the Somme could be the 'last push' which would lead to the decisive breakthrough. He miscalculated badly. The events of the next five months – the duration of the Somme offensive – would make Haig a reviled figure although, more recently, historians have taken a more benign view of the man.

Above: 30 June 1916 The calm before the storm. Two infantrymen share a quiet moment on the eve of the Somme offensive, which was to go down as the worst day in British military history.

Left: The Somme battlefield a week after the offensive was launched. Haig's resolve remained unshaken despite the heavy casualties suffered in those first few days.

Haig miscalculates

Haig believed that the artillery bombardment which launched the Somme offensive would obliterate every living thing on the 11-mile front and that his men - mostly 'Kitchener's Army' of volunteers - would stroll across across the enemy line with hardly a need for a rifle. The seeds of disaster had already been sown. Haig chose to double the depth of the bombardment from 1,250 to 2,500 yards but with the same number of shells, inevitably diluting its effectiveness. The bombardment failed to break Germany's first line of defence, the barbed wire, instead merely churning it into a dense entanglement. The explosives did produce a vast number of craters and they would present a further obstacle to troops burdened with 60lb. packs.

Above: Despite the huge casualties sustained in the early days of the Battle of the Somme, some gains were made by the Allies. Here a Tommy keeps watch in a captured German trench while some of his comrades rest.

Worst day in British military history

Far from being wiped out in the artillery bombardment that opened the Somme offensive, the German soldiers were ensconced in trenches that were up to 40ft. deep and survived relatively unscathed. When the guns fell silent and the order to advance was given, at 7:30a.m. on 1 July 1916, German troops emerged and manned the machine guns. What they saw was thousands of slow-moving infantry advancing in broad daylight. It was carnage. 100,000 men were deployed on the first day of the battle. By nightfall 60,000 were dead, wounded or missing, the worst disaster in British military history.

Above: German casualties in a trench taken by the Allies, 11 July 1916. The ferocious artillery bombardment which preceded the Somme offensive did not kill every living thing, however, as Haig had anticipated.

Left: The wasteland of the Somme.

Above: Lord Kitchener on a visit to the trenches during the Gallipoli campaign.

Field Marshal Horatio Kitchener

Kitchener had almost 40 years of military experience at the outbreak of the First World War. Kitchener was one of the few who had the prescience to see that the war would not be over quickly and that it would be won and lost on land. When the British Expeditionary Force was all but wiped out at Mons, the Marne and the First Battle of Ypres, Kitchener launched a recruitment campaign which resulted in over 2 million volunteers enlisting before conscription was finally introduced in 1916. The most celebrated recruiting poster showed the bewhiskered Kitchener himself urging men to join up.

Above: On 5 June 1916 Lord Kitchener was killed when his ship was sunk off the Orkney Islands. He had been on his way to Russia for talks. The *Daily Mail* published an announcement from Admiral Sir John Jellicoe, Commander-in-Chief of the Grand Fleet, which read:

'I have to report with deep regret that his Majesty's ship *Hampshire* (Captain Herbert J. Savill, RN), with Lord Kitchener and his staff on board, was sunk last night about 8pm to the west of the Orkneys, either by a mine or torpedo. ... As the whole shore has been searched from the seaward I greatly fear that there is little hope of there being any survivors. No report has yet been received from the search party on shore.'

Above: A panoramic view of Dompierre, which was completely destroyed during the Battle of the Somme.

Right: 31 July 1916. Highlanders at the front line, marching to the accompaniment of bagpipes. By the end of July the Allies had advanced just 2 miles on a narrow front.

Above: Preparing for battle behind the front line. Like many leaders, Haig, a former cavalryman with his military roots in the nineteenth century, had to come to terms with a very different style of combat in the First World War.

Left: Waiting for the order to advance. Not all soldiers shared Haig's optimism about the Somme offensive. Some took the opportunity to write their last letters home. There were also incidents of self-inflicted injury.

Above: The Allied attack on Fricourt was one of the few early successes at the Somme. It fell on 2 July 1916.

Left: 8-inch Howitzers deployed in the Fricourt-Mametz Valley, August 1916. The Allies used over 400 heavy guns at the Somme, one for every 60 yards of the front on which the attack took place.

Falkenhayn dismissed after failure at Verdun

On 4 June 1916 General Alexei Brusilov launched a huge offensive in Galicia. The Austro-Hungarian army was soon in disarray and there was an immediate call for reinforcements from the west. Three weeks later the British began the long-awaited attack on the Somme. Falkenhayn responded to these crises by scaling back the Verdun operation. In August he paid the price of failure, replaced as supreme commander of the German army by General von Hindenburg.

Above: Allied troops in the devastated town of Arras, which had been one of the early objectives of the Somme offensive.

Above: British troops attacking under artillery fire, 4 September 1916. By now the Battle of the Somme was a series of strikes and counter-strikes with heavy losses on both sides.

Left: British troops leaving their trenches at Morval, 4 September 1916.

Previous page: Reinforcements moving up towards Flers. They are seen crossing a German trench which was taken on 15 September.

Above: Infantry exposed to enemy fire on the open ground of the Somme battlefield. Of the 60,000 casualties on the first day of the offensive 90 per cent were claimed by German Maxim machine guns.

Left: Attacking behind a smokescreen at the Battle of the Somme. Haig remained convinced that a breakthrough was not only possible but imminent.

Battlefield debut for tanks

Some modest gains were made at the start of the Somme offensive, particularly by French units, but there was no breakthrough. Haig pressed on. For five months his single-minded determination led him to believe that the next attack would tip the balance. On 15 September he finally had tanks at his disposal. 49 were immediately deployed at the front, although many broke down before they even made it to no-man's-land. Those that reached the enemy line terrified the German soldiers but it was too soon for this new technology to make a telling difference in battle.

Above: Canadians go over the top, but this time the advance is aided by the appearance of tanks on the battlefield for the first time. The village of Courcelette was taken comfortably as this new armoured monster terrified German soldiers.

Right: A soldier cautiously checks a derelict building on all fours.

Left: Shell holes filled with water could be used for bathing. During the battle many wounded soldiers drowned in such craters.

Below: The strategically important Delville Wood was taken by a South African brigade in a ferocious six-day battle in July 1916. Only 750 of the 3,000-strong force had survived by the time relief arrived on 20 July.

Canadian infantry on their way to the front line, 10 October 1916. A combination of difficult terrain and mechanical unreliability meant that the tank was unable to give the Allies the vital edge. Haig was impressed enough to place an order for 1,000 tanks but that was for the future; in October and November 1916 more and more men were fed into the mincing machine of the Somme.

Right: A British officer watches as German trenches near Leuze Wood are shelled.

Below: Looking for signs of enemy activity from a captured trench, 15 September 1916. On 27 September the village of Thiepval was taken; it had been among the first-day objectives of the battle.

Paul von Hindenburg

Field Marshal Paul von Hindenburg was a veteran of Germany's victorious war with France in 1870-71. 68-year-old von Hindenburg was brought out of retirement almost as soon as war broke out, with Erich Ludendorff as his Chief-of-Staff. Von Hindenburg immediately led the 8th army to victory over Russian forces at Tannenberg, elevating him to hero status in his homeland. He was made Supreme Commander of the German army in August 1916, replacing Erich von Falkenhayn who fell from grace following the failed Verdun offensive.

Above: Delville Wood, renamed 'Devils Wood' by British soldiers. At the height of the battle German shells had rained down at a rate of 400 a minute, resulting in almost total deforestation.

Above: Reserves moving up to support the advance on Morval. This was one of the number of tiny parcels of land which both the British and German armies attacked or defended in great numbers and at great cost.

Above: An ammunition wagon struggles to negotiate the lunar landscape of the Somme battlefield. Conditions were infinitely worse after heavy rainfall.

Left: Allied troops at Longueval, which was taken as a precursor to the attack on Delville Wood, July 1916.

Above: A build-up of traffic on the muddy roads around the Somme. The graves of German soldiers can be seen on the right.

Left: The French drafted in Chinese munitions workers to free the country's own sons for front-line duty.

Longest battle of the war

In the autumn of 1916 the French reclaimed virtually all the territory they had lost at Verdun, including Ford Vaux and Fort Douaumont. The Battle of Verdun had lasted ten months, the longest of the entire war. It claimed almost one million casualties and at its conclusion in December 1916 the battle lines were hardly different from when the first shots were fired on 21 February.

Above: Verdun, 26 October 1916. French troops outside a pock-marked Fort Douaumont, which had just been retaken from the Germans.

Left: A British provincial town being combed for men who might be avoiding military service. Conscription meant that men were liable to be called up 30 days after their 18th birthday.

Above: Injured men are wheeled to makeshift hospitals to receive treatment and recuperate. There weren't anywhere near enough beds to accommodate the huge number of casualties. Base hospitals for the more serious cases were set up behind the lines and over 2 million injured men were repatriated for treatment during the course of the war. Many of the soldiers were treated for illness rather than battlefield injuries — influenza, malaria and pneumonia were common and thousands were hospitalised because of trenchfoot.

Above: 11 November 1916. Men of the Worcester regiment take a well-earned rest on a mudbank. Two days later Beaumont Hamel was taken, another first-day objective in Haig's original plan for the Somme offensive.

Left: The reserves of Kitchener's Army were seriously depleted in the battles of the Western Front in 1916. In May, just four months after the introduction of conscription, married men were also liable to be called up.

Above: The village of Bucquoy lies in ruins, destroyed in the Battle of the Ancre. This was the final phase of the Somme offensive, launched 13 November 1916.

Left: The Somme campaign of 1916 was a series of partial victories rather than the great breakthrough that had been envisaged and hoped for. The artillery bombardments meant that any gains made were invariably patches of wasteland and rubble.

Previous page: Troops outside their dugouts, Bazentin-le-Petit, July 1916.

Above: The barren landscape of the Somme battlefield. Nowhere did the Allies advance more than 6 miles from the line they held on 1 July. Losses amounted to 600,000, with German casualties reaching 400,000.

Above: One of the recruitment strategies was to allow groups of friends to serve together. All too often the so-called 'Pals Battalions' fell together and entire towns and villages could find themselves united in grief. The 11th Battalion of the East Lancashire Regiment, known as the Accrington Pals, was one of the worst hit on the first day of the Somme. Out of a force of around 700 men, 585 were reported dead or injured in one day.

Above: Stretcher-bearers transport a Canadian infantryman to safety. Many conscientious objectors volunteered for this dangerous non-combat job where the casualty rate was high. Others served as cooks or labourers. Until 1916 it was not compulsory for conscientious objectors to enrol in the military but following the introduction of conscription they were drafted and were court-martialled if they refused to cooperate.

The Somme battlefield takes on an eerily bleak quality as winter brings a brief hiatus to hostilities. Haig believed his decisions had been made with Divine guidance. He was made Field Marshal on 1 January 1917.

Above: The 51st Highland
Division took Beaumont Hamel
on 13 November 1916, one of
the final successes before Haig
closed the Somme offensive
down.

Right: A memorial to the
Germans who fell when the
Allies captured Beaumont Hamel.
The onset of winter forced Haig
to suspend the offensive five
days after the town fell.

Left: The site of Beaumont Hamel's church is reduced to mere rubble.

Below: The end of the four-and-a-half-month offensive brings temporary respite to the troops. Haig and Joffre planned a fresh initiative for the new year.

Somme claims one million casualties

It was the onset of winter that finally caused Haig to close down the Somme offensive. By the time that decision was taken, on 19 November, there had been one million casualties, two-thirds of them on the Allies' side. The territorial gain was just 6 miles. Bapaume, a first-day objective, was still 4 miles away when the offensive ended. All that flourished on the battlefield were poppies, which would become an enduring symbol of the appalling losses on the Somme and in future conflicts.

Left: The Western Front, 27 December 1916. German soldiers lie where they have fallen, while Allied artillery continues to pound the enemy lines. Historian A.J.P. Taylor said that 'idealism perished on the Somme'.

Above: The River Ancre, pictured a month after the Somme offensive ended there. The battles of 1916 hit both sides hard. In December of that year Germany made overtures for a peace settlement, while at the same time calling up every able-bodied man between 17 and 64 for war service. Germany suggested that the Allies could expect heavy defeats in 1917. Compromise on German terms was unconscionable after the year's heavy losses, even for war-weary Britain and France.

Left: A corrugated iron shed and brazier provide shelter and warmth for one British Tommy.

Below: Troops negotiating frozen ponds of muddy water on the Western Front, December 1916. The Somme campaign was a watershed in that volunteers and conscripts alike began to question the wisdom of their military and political masters. A mood of disillusionment, captured by war poets such as Wilfred Owen and Siegfried Sassoon, replaced the bullish, patriotic fervour of the first two years of war. This mood pervaded the armies of all the combatants and would manifest itself in 1917.

Right: British soldiers raise
a glass for King and
Country, Christmas 1916.

Below: For these soldiers,
Christmas lunch 1916
meant bread, jam and tea
consumed in a shell
crater at the graveside of
one of their comrades.

Entertainment at the front line

Trench warfare inevitably meant long periods of inactivity, even boredom. The men occupied themselves with sporting competitions, put on their own variety shows and eventually even had access to movies. These were important as a release valve from the pressures of life at the front, when any day could be a soldier's last. They gave a semblance of normality and helped raise morale.

Above: British soldiers negotiate with a French market trader for some mistletoe for their billet. Any semblance of home life, however small, helped to raise spirits.

Left: On 15 December 1916, a month after the end of the Somme campaign, the Battle of Verdun also finally came to an end. Casualties for the two great battles of 1916 amounted to 1.75 million – and still there was deadlock. In both Britain and France there was friction between the military and political leaders, the latter determined that 1917 should not see losses on such a scale for so little gain.

Periscopes were used for risk-free
observation from entrenched positions.

CHAPTER FOUR

Desperate Measures

The beginning of the new year saw Woodrow Wilson, recently elected for a second presidential term, still fighting to keep the USA out of the war. Wilson invited the belligerents to state the terms on which hostilities could end. The Central Powers offered no reply. The Allies' response, issued on 10 January 1917, stated that the aggressors, whose conduct had been 'a constant challenge to humanity and civilization', had to evacuate all territories that had been invaded and pay substantial reparations. Despite the Entente Powers' reaffirmation of a commitment to 'peace on those principles of liberty, justice and inviolable fidelity to international obligations', Wilson's decision was far from clear cut. He was wary of hegemony in any form, and although the Central Powers had violated sovereign territory, Britain and France were themselves great imperialist powers. Altruism would play no part in the President's decision making. Wilson wanted whatever was in America's best interest and knew that it might be necessary to commit to war in order to shape the peace.

AMERICA JOINS THE ENTENTE
Even after Germany launched its plan of unrestricted submarine warfare on 1 February 1917, Wilson would not be drawn into the war. America severed diplomatic relations with the Reich, but for the next two months the country pursued a policy of 'armed neutrality'. In March, three US cargo ships were sunk and the pressures increased. But for many Americans the final straw was an attempt by Germany to capitalise on long-standing grievances held by Mexico towards their country. Germany's Foreign Secretary, Arthur Zimmerman, sent a telegram to Mexico offering support for action to reclaim territory lost to America

in the previous century, including Arizona and Texas. The telegram was intercepted by the Allies and its contents revealed. There was a backlash across America and those previously wedded to an isolationist stance became pro-war in large numbers.

Wilson went to Congress to seek approval for a declaration of war on 2 April; the decision was ratified four days later. Even then Wilson studiously avoided the term 'ally'. The USA had thrown in her lot with the Entente Powers but would not be a signatory to the Pact of London, the agreement which bound the Allies to act in concert and not to conclude separate peace deals.

The formal declaration of war on 6 April was more a psychological than a military watershed. It would be some considerable time before the USA would be able to make a telling contribution to the fighting, something which Germany's high command was gambling on. Hindenburg and Ludendorff, sceptical about the chances of victory on the Western Front, put their faith in the U-boats. On land they would play a defensive game; at sea the German submarines, now unrestricted in their choice of targets, would crush Britain while America was still gearing up for war.

THE SIEGFRIED LINE
Germany's plan involved a withdrawal on the Western Front. In September 1916 work had begun on a new defensive line, one which would shorten the front by some thirty miles and provide, correspondingly, a welcome reduction in demand for resources. German forces withdrew to the Siegfried Line — or Hindenburg Line as the Allies would call it — in the early months of 1917. One thousand square miles of land —

territory which had been fought over so bitterly and with so much bloodshed – was conceded virtually at a stroke. As they withdrew, the Germans executed a comprehensive scorched-earth policy. The ground ceded to the Allies would have no useful resource, not even a drop of water, as all available supplies were poisoned.

Long before the Allies became aware of the German withdrawal they had met to plan their own strategy for 1917. Initially it was to be more of the same: concerted offensives on all fronts to stretch the enemy forces to the limit. That carried the prospect of another Somme, however, the spectre of which haunted Lloyd George. In the event a change in France's command structure dramatically altered the Allies' thinking, much to the British Prime Minister's relief. General Robert Nivelle replaced Joffre as Commander-in-Chief of the French Army in December 1916. Nivelle had distinguished himself at the Battle of the Marne and Verdun and his stock was so high that he had little difficulty in carrying the political leaders with him, not least because he told them exactly what they wanted to hear. Nivelle's plan was for an Anglo-French spring offensive on the Aisne. Saturation bombardments would be followed by a 'creeping barrage', behind which the infantry would advance. A

Below: The political leaders were determined that in 1917 there would be no repeat of the carnage that had occurred at Verdun and the Somme.

decisive breakthrough would be achieved within days. Haig was among the dissenting voices to this scheme but Lloyd George's approval meant his hands were tied.

SPRING OFFENSIVE

By the time the offensive got under way, on 9 April, it had already been undermined by Germany's withdrawal to the Hindenburg Line. Undaunted, Nivelle pressed on. There was early encouragement as the British attacked Arras and the Canadian Corps took Vimy Ridge, but when the main thrust came it proved to be yet another false dawn. The French army sustained over 100,000 casualties in the attack on Champagne. To make matters worse the strict time limit that had been imposed to achieve victory fell by the wayside. On 15 May Nivelle paid the price, replaced by General Pétain. This alone was not enough for the French infantry, however. After more failed promises and more mass slaughter they had had enough and there was mutiny on a mass scale. Had the German Army been aware of the situation an easy victory might have been had.

Pétain responded with a mixture of carrot and stick. The offensive was called off and conditions on the front line were improved. On the other hand anarchy could not go unpunished and 23 mutineers faced a firing squad 'pour encourager les autres'.

Privation, hardship and mass slaughter for no discernible gain would provoke dissent in the ranks of all the major combatants. Everywhere the consensus required to prosecute the war seemed in danger of breaking down and all leaders recognised that the morale of both troops and civilians needed careful monitoring. In Russia, dissent spilled over into full-blown revolution: the winter of 1916-17 saw both Russia's Army and her people at breaking point. Poorly fed, ill-equipped and badly led, the troops refused to

fight. The civilian population was faced with dwindling food supplies and soaring prices. On 8 March workers in Petrograd went on strike and took to the streets. Unlike 1905, when a similar uprising had been brutally put down, the troops' sympathies lay with the protestors. The Duma announced that it no longer recognised the Tsar, who abdicated on 15 March.

A moderate provisional government was established but the seeds of a second revolution were already sown. Exiled revolutionaries, including Lenin, returned to Russia determined to take advantage of the fact that the country was in a state of flux. Germany was only too pleased to assist his passage, quick to realise the value of internecine strife in the enemy camp. And it was Russia's involvement in the war which became the key issue. The provisional government believed that the war still had to be won; the Bolshevik revolutionaries wanted an immediate end to a conflict which was seen as a product of capitalism and imperialism.

BOLSHEVIKS SEIZE POWER

Russia's allies and enemies waited. The House of Commons sent a message of 'heartfelt congratulations' to the Duma. It was hoped that with a new democratic structure Russia would prosecute the war with 'renewed steadfastness'. In June 1917 she tried to do just that,

with disastrous consequences. A failed offensive in Galicia left Russian soldiers believing they were no better off under a post-Tsarist regime. There was desertion on a mass scale. On 7 November – 26 October in Russia, which was still operating on the Julian calendar – the Bolsheviks seized power with minimal resistance.

The events in Russia in 1917 were not only the consequence of disaffection with war but also served to feed it. By the summer of 1917 there was also great discontent in the ranks of the Italian army. In August Italy launched its eleventh unsuccessful offensive against Austro-Hungarian forces across the Isonzo river. General Cadorna's army had sustained huge losses in these campaigns in the north-east of the country, but the twelfth was to prove even more devastating. The disintegration of the Russian Army meant that German troops were able to be deployed to aid their allies. Ludendorff masterminded the twelfth battle of the Isonzo, in which the Central Powers aimed to break through the Italian line near Caporetto.

The offensive began on 24 October 1917 with a heavy artillery bombardment,

Below Men who had hitherto been exempt from conscription received their call-up papers in January 1917. Canada, a country which had provided a substantial volunteer contingent, also finally introduced conscription.

Above: Georges Clemenceau (second left) became France's prime minister in 1917. Even at the age of 76 he was formidably belligerent. 'I wage war!' was his watchword.

mainly of gas shells against which the standard issue Italian masks were largely ineffective. Even so, General Otto von Below, who led the attack, could hardly have imagined the ease with which his infantry were able to advance. The Italian Army was soon on the retreat. In freezing conditions ten regiments chose surrender instead. Crumbling morale had once again provoked mutinous action. Italian machinery for dealing with indiscipline was the severest of all, yet here was further proof that the military and political leaders could no longer take unquestioning loyalty for granted.

The Central powers did not escape their share of rebelliousness. The Allies' blockade meant shortages and hardship both in Austria-Hungary and Germany. There was civil unrest but for now this did not spread to the armed forces on any significant scale. To forestall that eventuality, Ludendorff instigated a programme in which the troops were invited to restate their love for the Fatherland and their unswerving desire for victory.

THE BATTLE OF PASSCHENDAELE

After the disastrous Nivelle spring offensive, the French were in no position to instigate a fresh attack on the Western Front. But Haig, his authority restored, was determined to do just that. His plan was to break through the German line at Ypres and push through to the Belgian coast, cutting off the enemy's right flank. This would also put the Allies within striking distance of the German submarine bases at Ostend and Zeebrugge. The Entente Powers were deeply concerned by Germany's U-boat policy and any action which could harm that operation was an attractive proposition. Lloyd George was still concerned about the ghastly prospect of another Somme. Pétain was also sceptical. He favoured a defensive operation until America could mobilise in numbers. With the cracks in the French Army still not healed and America a long way from battle-readiness, Haig saw the chance of a glorious victory for the British Expeditionary Force. He got his wish and plans for the third Battle of Ypres — or Passchendaele, as it would come to be known — got under way.

The first target was the Messines Ridge, a key vantage point to the south of Ypres which had been held by the Germans for two years. General Sir Herbert Plumer led the successful attack on the ridge on 7 June. Preparations for the main assault could now proceed unhindered and unobserved. Six weeks passed between the taking of the Messines Ridge and the launch of the main offensive, a delay which the Germans put to good use. The bombardment, when it came, churned up ground whose drainage system had long since collapsed. To make matters worse, the rains were early and heavy, and in the advance the British soldiers had to contend with thick mud and water-filled craters as well as enemy fire. The Germans had already abandoned the idea of entrenched positions in such conditions, choosing instead to defend with machine guns housed in pillboxes. It would be another month before the weather improved and the Allies gained a sight of Passchendaele Ridge, which had been among the first-day objectives. In October the rains returned but Haig remained unshakeable, seduced by the desire to capture Passchendaele and the belief that the German Army was about to crack. Passchendaele did finally fall, on 2 November, though at enormous cost. More than 250,000 casualties had been sustained in an advance of just five miles. The German Army had not been vanquished, while Zeebrugge and Ostend continue to service the submarines that had been inflicting such grievous losses on Allied shipping.

FOUR HUNDRED TANKS ATTACK CAMBRAI

To keep up the momentum gained by taking Passchendaele the Allies launched one final offensive on the Western Front in 1917. The Battle of Cambrai, which began on 20 November, was notable for the number of tanks deployed. Over 400 spearheaded the attack, the first time tanks had been seen on a battlefield in such numbers. Encouraging early gains were made, but direct hits and mechanical breakdowns meant that tank numbers were depleted following the initial breakthrough. The German Army countered and the inevitable stalemate was soon restored.

A year beset by difficulties for the Allies ended on a somewhat brighter note when news came through that Field Marshal Allenby's Egyptian Expeditionary Force had captured Beersheba and Gaza before marching into Jerusalem on 9 December. But on the main fronts there was little to celebrate: the Nivelle fiasco and Passchendaele in the west, Caporetto in Italy and complete collapse in the east following the Russian Revolution. The total war waged by German U-boats, which had been devastating in the early months, had been mitigated somewhat by the use of the convoy system, whereby merchant ships travelled together, under the protection of warships. Rationing was introduced into Britain at the end of 1917, a measure to which even the King and Queen succumbed. However, Germany's attempt to bring Britain to her knees had failed. 1918 held out the prospect of the American Expeditionary Force led by General John Pershing becoming a key player on the Western Front, as recruits and conscripts completed their training and became ready for frontline duty. Germany had won the battle in the east but it was she who was living on borrowed time.

Below: Russian soldiers in Toulon, from where they were bound for the Western front. A tide of disaffection swept through the Russian army and people in 1917, with dramatic consequences.

Above: Migrant labour engaged in construction work in France. The new year saw a new man in command of the French army. Joffre was replaced by Robert Nivelle, who won the admiration and trust of the politicians by his distinguished efforts in the defence of Verdun.

Right: A pine forest in Lorraine is interlaced with barbed wire to hold up any German attack.

Left: Soldiers often had to put up with an amphibious lifestyle on the Western front.

Below: British soldiers carrying stove pipes during the harsh winter of 1916-17.

Above: Conditions in the winter of 1916-17 were severe for the Allies, even more so for Germany. Under the Hindenburg Programme, increasingly scarce resources were geared towards the war effort. German people lacked basic provisions during this period, which became ingrained in the memory as the 'turnip winter'.

Right: The chateau at Gommencourt, destroyed by the German army during the retreat to the Hindenburg Line, which began on 24 February 1917. The Germans adopted a scorched earth policy as they withdrew to a new defensive position.

Left: Soldiers were billeted in Nissen huts, which were portable and convenient forms of accommodation. They were named after their designer, British mining engineer Lieutenant-Colonel Peter Nissen.

Below: A Nissen hut encampment.

General Joseph Joffre

Sixty-two-year-old Joffre was Commander-in-Chief of French forces at the outbreak of war. He initially fell into the German trap of moving the bulk of his men to Alsace-Lorraine. Joffre believed in attacking with speed and spirit – the famous French élan – which had such catastrophic consequences in the early days of the war. He salvaged his reputation by pulling back in time to halt the German army when it was on the brink of taking Paris. Victory at the Battle of the Marne was the final nail in the coffin of the Schlieffen Plan and put 'Papa' Joffre on a pedestal as far as the French people were concerned. When the war developed into an entrenched stalemate, Joffre's lack of imagination was exposed, although the stresses never prevented him from taking hearty meals and daytime naps. He was replaced by Robert Nivelle in December 1916.

Above: February 1917. The snow-covered battlefield of the Somme, where so many had fallen just a few months earlier. The Allies' plan going into 1917 was for a renewed offensive here, combined with fresh initiatives on both the Eastern Front and Italy, a concerted effort to squeeze the Central Powers.

Left: Bapaume ablaze as Allied troops march into the town, 21 March 1917.

Below: Ludendorff had planned the withdrawal to the Hindenburg Line in September 1916 but it would not be completed until March of the following year. The retreat shortened the German line by some 25 miles, freeing 14 divisions.

Right: Bapaume, 21 March 1917. British troops on the banks of a vast crater, where a mine had exploded shortly before they entered the town.

Below: The German army made sure that the savings gained by withdrawing to the Hindenburg Line would not be offset by giving the enemy access to any useful resources. The Allies entered Peronne to find it razed to the ground.

Above: German soldiers left a note on Peronne's town hall, which had served as their headquarters. It read: 'Don't be angry, just be amazed'.

Above: Allied troops in pursuit of the retreating enemy. The Hindenburg Line was a misnomer: it comprised four separate zones which gave a formidable defence up to four miles deep in places.

Right: Crossing the River Somme near Peronne. The rapid gains which the German withdrawal afforded the Allies were short-lived; 1917 would see more attritional battles on a scale approaching those of the previous year.

Lawrence of Arabia

Thomas Edward Lawrence was an academic who had travelled widely in the Middle East engaged in archaeological study. When war broke out Lawrence was a junior intelligence officer, and he helped devise a plan to incite Arab resistance against Turkish rule. With his knowledge of Arab culture Lawrence was given the role of liaising with the Arab leaders, to whom he became an idol. He masterminded and took part in a highly successful guerrilla campaign, notably the attacks on the Hijaz railway. Arab leaders believed the quid pro quo for their contribution towards an Allied victory would be the establishment of an independent Arab state, a vision also cherished by Lawrence. These ambitions were shattered in the post-conflict agreements.

Above: 'No road this way'. The German legacy to the pursuing enemy in February-March 1917 was difficult access routes and derelict buildings.

Right: The inhabitants of a village formerly under German occupation welcome a contingent of British soldiers.

Above: Sappers quickly constructed new bridges to replace those left in ruins by the Germans.

US angered by Zimmerman telegram

In February and March 1917 several American ships were sunk by German U-boats. The USA was further angered by a telegram sent by Germany's foreign minister, Arthur Zimmerman, to the Mexican government. Germany attempted to exploit long-standing territorial grievances between Mexico and the US, and offered support for a Mexican invasion of her northern neighbour. The telegram was intercepted by the Allies and its contents revealed to the Wilson government. It was another factor in persuading the US president to abandon his country's neutral stance and enter the war on the Allies' side.

Above: An Anzac patrol in Bapaume, 29 March 1917. By now von Hindenburg and Ludendorff had put their faith in unrestricted submarine warfare as a way to achieve a swift victory.

Left and Below: 'Vive Tommie!' French villagers come out on to the streets to greet the men seen as delivering them from German oppression. Their euphoria was in contrast to the growing feelings of disillusionment felt among French *poilus*. Within weeks there would be concerted disobedience in the French army after yet another disastrous offensive. Five hundred death sentences were ordered, though only 50 were carried out.

Right: The German army removed the statue from this plinth in Bapaume and replaced it with a dummy anti-aircraft weapon. An Anzac soldier takes the opportunity to record his name for posterity.

Below: Noyon, 30 March 1917. Local residents queueing for basic provisions. Towns under German occupation had all their resources commandeered for the war effort.

Above: Bapaume, viewed from the town hall, 30 March 1917.

War in the Air

By 1915 aircraft were being fitted with machine guns to increase their attacking capability. For the pilot the best place to site such a weapon was in his direct eyeline straight ahead, but the plane's propellers presented an obstacle. The French introduced a deflector mechanism, by which the bullets that would have hit the propellers were prevented from doing so. It worked but was wasteful of ammunition. The Germans stole a march when Anthony Fokker developed 'interrupter gear' which synchronized the firing of the bullets with the rotation of the propeller. For a short time the Fokker monoplane reigned supreme and inflicted heavy casualties. Parity was restored when the Allies developed a similar mechanism.

USA declares war

On 6 April 1917
Woodrow Wilson gained
the approval of Congress
for the USA to enter the
war. For three years he had
maintained the country's
neutrality, even in the face
of acts of aggression
which included the sinking
of the *Lusitania*. When
Germany adopted a policy
of unrestricted submarine
warfare on 1 February
1917, its leaders knew
that there was a strong
likelihood that the USA
would be drawn into the
conflict. The Central
Powers gambled on
delivering a knockout blow
to its European enemies
before US forces could
mobilize.

Above: An Anzac marching
band plays against a
backdrop of smoke and
embers.

Right: Returning to the
battlefield, April 1917.
General Robert Nivelle
conceived the idea for a
grand spring offensive on
the Aisne. His military
credentials were such that
he carried the day with his
ambitious plan.

Above: The British launched an attack at Arras on 9 April 1917, a diversionary operation in advance of the main offensive on the Aisne.

Left: British soldiers returning to the trenches at Arras. The first day of the battle was a triumph for the Allies. The German line was penetrated by up to 3 miles and the Canadian Corps took Vimy Ridge, all with few casualties sustained.

Above: Limbers pass through the ruins of Athies during the Battle of Arras. After initial gains, which were as spectacular as any seen on the Western Front for two years, the German army countered effectively.

Above: Vigilance and relaxation in a forward trench. The German army was initially under strength at Arras and Vimy. When reserves arrived the battle took on a familiar pattern of grim attrition.

Above: Jubilant British soldiers after the impressive start of the Arras campaign.

Right: The battlefield around Vimy. The offensive lost its impetus as exhausted Allied troops paused to recover. Meanwhile German reinforcements quickly arrived to shore up their defences.

Prostitution rife

With the exception of nurses, women played no part in front-line duty. For the music-hall-style entertainment British soldiers donned wigs and dresses for the female roles. With such concentrations of men prostitution was rife. Commanding officers in the French and German armies generally accepted the inevitability of this and simply tried to ensure that venereal disease was kept in check.

Above: A corner of the battlefield at Arras. Tanks were on hand and were deployed during an attempt by Australian troops to break through at Bullecourt. They failed to get past the wire defences and from this point the pendulum of the spring offensive swung in Germany's favour.

Right: The slopes of Vimy
Ridge pitted with shell craters.
In a single assault Canadian
troops took the ridge, where so
many French soldiers had
perished in 1915.

Below: A family home in Arras is
exposed as the external wall has
been destroyed through shelling.

Above: Troops are taken by bus for rest and recovery after heavy fighting at Arras.

Right: The chateau at Caulicourt, reduced to rubble by German explosives.

Below: Mending a puncture under shellfire. The cycling corps provided an invaluable line of communication, especially in conditions where animals and motor vehicles were liable to struggle.

Life in the trenches

Even when soldiers were not under fire conditions in the trenches were brutal. There were infestations of rats, lice and fleas. Soldiers had to live with being wet and cold, which made cases of trench foot common. Oral hygiene was not high on the list of priorities, and teeth and gums were prone to bacterial infection, known as trench mouth. Men also had to become inured to going about their daily business next to corpses and limbs of dismembered bodies. Such conditions brought gallows humour to the fore. This may not have raised spirits but at least it tried to ensure they weren't completely crushed.

Above: Silhouetted figures of Highland troops embarking on a dawn attack.

Above: Canadian
troops acknowledge
their triumphant
attack on Vimy
Ridge, a strategic
vantage point which
gave the Allies a
panoramic view of
enemy positions on
the Douai plain.

Above: 17 May 1917. The ruins of Pozieres, with an abandoned German trench in the foreground.

Left: Cavalry on the move, 31 May 1917. Cavalry was used at the beginning of the war in fighting and for scouting. But by 1917 Britain and France had lost over half a million horses. Road and rail had taken over as the main methods of transportation and some cavalry units were fighting on foot.

The British offensive should have ended by now but Haig was forced to prolong the operation as the main attack by the French at Chemin des Dames was going disastrously.

Above: Loading ammunition wagons, early June 1917. By now Nivelle's grand offensive on the Aisne was a shattered dream. Nivelle himself was replaced by Philippe Pétain on 29 April 1917.

Spectacular explosion at Messines Ridge

As a precursor to the main offensive at Ypres in spring 1917 the Allies detonated 19 huge mines around Messines Ridge, a strategic point to the south-east of the main target which had been in German hands since the autumn of 1914. One million pounds of explosive produced a spectacular conflagration and in the ensuing chaos Haig's men took the ridge with ease. Instead of pressing home the advantage by immediately targeting Ypres itself, Haig waited for six weeks. In that time King George V paid a visit to the front and was treated to a re-enactment of the successful attack on Messines Ridge. But the momentum was lost. The German army had time to recover, and then, worst of all, nature dealt Haig a cruel blow. The heavens opened, reducing the entire area to a quagmire.

Above: British troops in Arras, 7 June 1917. Haig's extended offensive to help take the pressure off the beleaguered French came at the cost of some 160,000 casualties. The French army sustained even greater losses in just ten days. It was the straw which pushed many *poilus* over the edge.

Above: Nivelle's spring offensive produced a landscape all too familiar on the Western Front. What it didn't produce was a breakthrough. Germany had some 40 divisions in place at the Aisne; Nivelle had nowhere near the numerical superiority needed to overcome a force of that strength.

From Field-Marshal Sir Douglas Haig

Thursday Morning.
'We attacked at 3.10 a.m. the German positions on the Messines-Wytschaete Ridge [south of Ypres] on a front of over 9 miles. We have everywhere captured our first objectives, and further progress is reported to be satisfactory along the whole front of attack.'

Daily Mail, 8 June 1917

Left: Statues from Arras Cathedral are rescued and laid out on stretchers in a church behind Allied lines.

Below: Allied troops in a German observation post at Messines Ridge. Nivelle's failed offensive led Haig to harbour thoughts of a fresh British initiative at Ypres.

Haig goes on the offensive

The Allies had taken Ypres in the early days of the war, when both sides were engaged in a 'race to the sea'. The Germans tried to capture the town in the spring of 1915, using chlorine gas for the first time on the Western Front. In the summer of 1917 Haig decided to go on the offensive, with the ultimate objective of reaching Zeebrugge and Ostend, the bases from where German U-boats were wreaking havoc on Allied shipping.

Above: Watching shell-burst near Bullecourt, 17 July 1917. Pétain, the new French commander, was preoccupied with trying to restore morale among his men. He advised a holding operation until American forces arrived in numbers. Haig chose to go on the offensive.

Right: A wiring party load a pack-horse in preparation for moving to the front.

Left: A company of Irish Guardsmen on the march, 7 August 1917. The Third Battle of Ypres – commonly known as Passchendaele – had been launched a week earlier.

Below: Hauling an 18-pound field gun out of glutinous mud. The summer and autumn of 1917 would be the wettest Flanders had seen in living memory.

Above: Pilckem, August
1917. The battlefields of
Flanders were also littered
with countless animal
carcasses.

Opposite: Rifle-cleaning after battle, August 1917. Haig
was buoyed by the successful raid on the Messines Ridge
in June and remained determined to see the Third Battle
of Ypres successfully prosecuted, even in the face of
heavy losses and adverse weather conditions.

First American Fighters

The first contingents of the troops which the United States is sending
to fight side by side with the armies of the Allies landed on French soil
this morning. The meeting between the American general in command of
the transports and the French officers on the quay was of a most
friendly character. The general, a veteran of the Cuban, Philippine and
Mexican campaigns said, 'I am happy to be the commander of the first
troops who will fight shoulder to shoulder with the heroes of the Marne
and Verdun.' The general then left to inspect the camp where his men
will be lodged.

Daily Mail, 28 June 1917

Lloyd George expresses doubts about Ypres attack

After the salutary lesson of the Somme many had grave reservations about further offensives on the Western Front, including Lloyd George. The British prime minister felt that with Russia's contribution uncertain and France seemingly in crisis Britain could ill afford to be profligate with resources. He favoured a holding operation in 1917, buying time until US forces could arrive in numbers. Haig disagreed. His instincts were always to attack, believing that the next push would be the straw that would break Germany's creaking back. To Haig, the very fact that Russia was in a state of flux and there was a crisis of morale in the French ranks made it all the more imperative for Britain to carry the fight to the enemy. Lloyd George still had misgivings but in the end deferred. He left the military men to take the decision, and the responsibility.

Left: Keeping both men and equipment dry in Flanders in the summer and autumn of 1917 was an impossible task. The vast muddy pools were not just an inconvenience but a potential death-trap.

Above: A crowded road at Fricourt, 18 August 1917. The latest Flanders offensive was in its third week. The casualties sustained were not on the scale of the Somme, yet the overall picture was the same: heavy loss for marginal gain.

Right: A soldier shields himself as a shell bursts nearby. The devastated landscape meant that once out of their trenches soldiers were cruelly exposed to enemy fire.

Above: Soldiers seemingly
at a loss as to how to
free a horse and its load
stuck fast in the
glutinous earth.

Right: Stretcher-bearers rescue a wounded soldier, early September 1917, when there was a brief respite from the monsoon conditions.

Below: Lancers making their way through the ruins of a French village, 22 September 1917.

'Bite and hold'

The battle that would come to be known as Passchendaele was launched at 3.50a.m. on 31 July, with Gheluvelt Plateau among the first targets, including the village of Passchendaele itself. Instead of trying to make a dramatic breakthrough the Allies now opted for more modest, piecemeal gains where the infantry advanced behind a curtain of artillery fire. This was the 'bite and hold' strategy which some senior officers had advised a year earlier at the Somme. One hundred and thirty-six tanks joined in the attack, but ground conditions nullified their contribution – a portent of what was to come.

Above: Undertaking maintenance work in trenches that were dry, temporarily at least. The German defences in Flanders were nine zones deep, some of the strongest on the entire Western Front.

Field Marshal Sir Douglas Haig

General Haig helped to establish the British Expeditionary Force in 1906, and he was a corps commander when the force landed in France in August 1914. By the end of the year he was in charge of the First Army and in December 1915 he took over from Sir John French as Commander-in-Chief of British forces, a position he held until the end of hostilities. Haig was a dour Scot, an old cavalryman whose tactical awareness, some believed, remained in the 19th century. His single-minded tenacity was regarded as both his strength and his weakness. Haig's determination to achieve a breakthrough in the Somme and the Ypres offensives, despite appalling casualties, would make him one of the war's most controversial figures. His detractors often overlook the series of victories he presided over in the final months of the war, which resulted in Germany's final capitulation.

Left: Stretcher-bearers at work in Flanders. The casualties sustained by the Allies were enough to prompt a concerned Lloyd George to recall Haig to London in early September. Once again the British prime minister felt unable to pull political rank over his senior military man.

Right: The German army's concrete pillboxes, housing machine guns, were formidable defensive strongholds. Direct hits were needed to neutralise them.

Below: A British soldier contemplates the state of battle from a captured machine-gun emplacement. As everywhere, morale was low in the British army in the autumn of 1917.

Above: Trees uprooted by shelling were used for road-making, bridges and strengthening dugouts.

Above: After a fine, dry September, in which important gains were made, the weather deteriorated dramatically in Flanders in October 1917.

Right: Some of Haig's senior generals advised a suspension of hostilities as the fields of Flanders were choked with mud. Haig resolutely decided to press forward.

Many drown as shell-holes fill with water

The German defences at Ypres were strong. Ground conditions meant that they were unable to build their usual cavernous trenches, but there was a network of concrete pillboxes containing machine-gun crews. The German commander, Crown Prince Rupprecht, chose his moment well to counter. The ground was now so churned up that many of the injured who struggled to reach a shell crater drowned as their place of sanctuary filled with water.

Above: 14 October 1917. One regiment marches while another rests. September's successes included the capture of Menin Road Ridge and Polygon Wood. However, it had taken over two months instead of the anticipated two days.

Right: 20 October 1917.
Soldiers being
transported to the front
for yet another 'last
push'. Once again Haig
believed that the
German army was
teetering on the brink
of collapse.

Below: Constructing
drainage channels to
clear away at least some
of the surface water.
The land drains had
long since been
destroyed by shelling.

Above: 12 October 1917. The corpses of German soldiers lie beside one of the many fortified strongholds the Allies had to face. On this day Anzac troops suffered heavy losses as they made the first attempt to take Passchendaele.

The cost of Passchendaele

Allied casualties in total for the Third Battle of Ypres were almost a quarter of a million. On the positive side Haig had certainly occupied the German army for four months when the French army was in a parlous state. However, he was not apprised of the extent of the mutinous behaviour among the *poilus*. Moreover, there is no indication that the German hierarchy had any notion of France's vulnerability in the summer of 1917. Passchendaele, a strategic irrelevance, thus became a byword for futile slaughter.

Left: Despite mounting casualties, which would total 250,000 for the entire campaign, Haig would not be deflected from his objective: Passchendaele Ridge and the village of Passchendaele itself.

Above: 28 October 1917.
Enjoying a brief rest after
an attack which had seen
Thiepval and Combles fall
to the Allies.

Right: 31 October 1917.
The day after yet another
attack on Passchendaele,
which had been repulsed
with the aid of mustard
gas.

Left: An evacuated German fort, which the soldiers had attempted to flood before retreating.

Below: Canadian troops marking out the ground for road construction. When the Canadian Corps finally took Passchendaele on 6 November 1917 it was little more than a mass of rubble.

Massed tank attack planned for Cambrai

Even as Passchendaele was limping towards a hollow victory the Allied leaders turned their thoughts to a new initiative. Every army to a lesser or greater extent was suffering from low morale in 1917, and Haig saw the need to reinvigorate his men with the prospect of a potentially decisive breakthrough. Cambrai was targeted, and the ace in the Allied attack was the Tank Corps. Tanks had already been used, in piecemeal fashion with patchy results. At Cambrai 300 tanks would be used to spearhead the attack.

Above: 17 November 1917. Haig belatedly realised that Passchendaele had been something of a Pyrrhic victory. He immediately set in train plans for a fresh morale-boosting set-piece offensive to be carried out before the end of the year.

Above: British cavalry on the move, 21 November 1917. A day earlier the Allies had launched the Battle of Cambrai, where tanks, not horses, would be in the vanguard.

Above: 24 November 1917. An
ammunition column stretches as
far as the eye can see. Initial gains
at the Battle of Cambrai, now
four days old, were impressive.

Right: Men of the East Anglian
regiment occupying a German
trench on the first day of the
Battle of Cambrai. Some
regiments counted their losses in
single figures, a far cry from the
kind of casualty rates that had
attended all previous Western
Front offensives.

Church bells ring out to celebrate success at Cambrai

For the Battle of Cambrai, Haig had the new Mark IV tank at his disposal. These were fitted with Lewis guns and some also had six-pounders. Just as importantly, they would also make short work of the thick barbed wire defences laid by the Germans. The attack was launched on 20 November 1917. There was no artillery bombardment beforehand, which would only have served as a signal to the enemy that an offensive was imminent. It was a stunning success. By midday the German line had been breached in several places. The only disappointment was at the centre of the 6-mile front, where the infantry lagged too far behind the tanks and left them exposed to German fire. Even so an advance of 5 miles in a day, at little cost, was a spectacular triumph compared with the bitter experience of the Somme and Ypres. Many Germans fled, others meekly surrendered. The church bells rang out in Britain in joyous celebration, the only time that had happened since the outbreak of war.

Above: Highland Territorials crossing a German communication trench during the attack on Flesquieres. The troops lagged too far behind the tanks in this area, however, allowing enemy forces to strike back effectively.

German army strikes back at Cambrai

If anything, the first day of the Battle of Cambrai went too well
for the Allies. The tanks had gained so much ground that there
were insufficient reserves to press home the advantage. The German
army countered. Some 170 tanks were disabled, either by enemy
fire or breakdown. The remaining tank crews were at the point of
exhaustion. With the tank threat now largely nullified the battle
reverted to a more typical exchange, and on 30 November 1917
German forces struck a savage blow and regained much of the lost
territory. At the end of the Battle of Cambrai the situation was
largely unaltered. The Tank Corps had brought the Allies close to
an important victory and shown that the German commanders had
been unwise to ignore this new technology.

Above: 29 November 1917.
Allied troops in former
enemy-occupied territory.
The following day the
Germans launched a huge
counter-offensive, winning
back much of the ground
they had ceded.

Above: Sentry duty in a heavily sandbagged lookout station. Note the warning sign: no imminent threat from a gas attack.

Right: A postbag from Blighty brings Christmas cheer. Jerusalem fell to the Allies on 9 December 1917 but after more than three years the balance of power on the Western Front was still delicately poised.

Below: All the warring nations experienced shortages of foodstuffs and essential resources. The unrestricted U-boat campaign began to bite in Britain, where rationing was finally introduced. The peoples of Germany and Austria-Hungary were also suffering severe privation.

Above: A brigadier-general acts as a waiter to troops on leave in Paris, 29 December 1917. That month the new Communist government in Russia signed an armistice with Germany; Britain and France had lost their major ally.

British soldiers resting on a mudbank, March 1918, the month in which the 'Kaiser's Battle' began, Germany's final, bold gamble to win the war.

CHAPTER FIVE

Victory At A Price

By the end of 1917 the German high command had little room for manoeuvre. It was clear that the U-boat threat had diminished and could not now be the instrument of victory. It was also clear that the condition of her army and civilians — and that of the other Central Powers — meant that war could not be waged for much longer. The Allied blockade was continuing to bite, and although it fell short of starving Germany into submission, it was causing suffering which would only be supportable in the short term. Hardship could be borne while there remained the prospect of a great military victory. Equally pressing was the fact that 1918 would bring American forces across the Atlantic in ever greater numbers. The Bolshevik Revolution provided a welcome fillip to Ludendorff and von Hindenburg for it brought an end to hostilities on the Eastern Front in December 1917. Although it would be another three months before a formal treaty between Germany and Russia was signed, at Brest-Litovsk on 3 March 1918, from the start of the year Germany's military leaders were able to plan their strategy with this in mind.

STORM TROOPERS DEPLOYED

In fact there was little to discuss. There had to be a deployment of troops from east to west, for it was in France and Belgium that Germany must play her final cards, and play them before US forces arrived in numbers. Operation Michael was conceived, a spring offensive around Arras which would shatter the Allied line and drive relentlessly northeastwards to the Channel coast. A new tactic would be employed. Instead of fixed objectives Ludendorff put his faith in a rapid infiltration of the enemy line by specially trained sturmtruppen or storm troops. Momentum was the key, and at all costs the Allies were to be given no breathing space to recover. It was a huge gamble. Up to one million men had had to remain in vanquished Russia and some of Germany's senior officers thought the plan far too ambitious. But it was a gamble virtually forced on Ludendorff. If he could drive a wedge between the British and French forces, victory might yet be salvaged from the jaws of defeat.

ALLIES WELCOME US

The Allies, by contrast, went into 1918 in a more defensive frame of mind. This was partly down to the reverses of the previous year. Lloyd George was wary of committing significant numbers of troops to Haig, whom he felt was too profligate with lives, too ready to embark on futile offensives. The Entente Powers also knew that time was on their side. And it wasn't only American troops that were eagerly awaited. The prosecution of the war had left Britain close to bankruptcy. The final bill would be £10 billion, of which some £7 billion was borrowed. By 1918 three-quarters of the country's national income was directed at the war effort; never before had the nation's resources been so overwhelmingly linked to a single undertaking. Such was the nature of total war. It meant that the financial backing of the US would be as welcome as her manpower and machinery.

Britain's situation remained a delicate one, however. In 1918 the number of days lost to strikes exceeded six million, an indication that the exhortation to show restraint in support of the war effort was wearing thin. In March the Defence of the Realm Act was amended to make it an offence for women to pass on sexually transmitted diseases to servicemen, the incidence of which was reaching epidemic proportions. The fact that this was made punishable by a heavy fine or imprisonment had more to do with the need to have men fit for active duty than any question of morality. As a hedge against future manpower needs, the 1918 Military Service Bill raised from 41 to 50 the age at which men were liable to be conscripted.

Woodrow Wilson did not wait for American resources to play a part in winning the war. On 8 January 1918 he delivered an address to Congress in which he outlined his ideas for post-conflict Europe. The famous 'Fourteen Points' speech envisioned a Europe of nations based on democracy and self-determination. States should be armed only insofar as to provide for domestic security. A League of Nations would oversee international relations and provide collective security. Wilson delivered the speech without consulting the Allies, and not all of his pronouncements would have been well received. Freedom of navigation on the seas, both in peace and in war, was a stipulation by which Britain, a great naval power, would have felt hamstrung. And the president's call for transparent pacts between governments was a far cry from the secret deals by which many of the minor combatants had been seduced to declare for one side or the other. However, Wilson knew he held a strong hand in January 1918 and was determined to be the prime mover in shaping the new world order.

Only 300,000 US troops had reached Europe by the time Operation Michael was launched, on 21 March. Meanwhile, trains had been transporting German troops from the east day and night for weeks. Although some used this huge logistical undertaking as

Below: The Council of Four, which made all the key decisions in the post-conflict treaties. Italy's prime minister Vittorio Emmanuele Orlando (left) was a marginal figure in the group, which effectively became the 'Big Three': Lloyd George, Clemenceau and Wilson.

an apposite moment to desert, Germany now had a numerical advantage on the Western Front for the first time since the opening months of the war. A last-ditch effort for victory posed a formidable threat.

The Allies suspected that an attack was imminent but did not know where or when. A heavy artillery bombardment, including the use of gas shells, announced the beginning of the offensive in the early hours of 21 March. The main point of attack was between Arras and St. Quentin, with the British Third and Fifth Armies bearing the brunt. The shelling then switched to a creeping barrage and the infantry began their advance. Initial gains were spectacular as waves of fresh troops joined the attack in a rolling spearhead, a tactic which maintained the vital forward momentum. The German army swept across the Somme battlefield and quickly took Peronne, Bapaume and Albert. Disagreement between Haig and Pétain regarding the Allies' response served the German army well. The assault threatened to separate the French and British, which could have had catastrophic consequences.

FOCH BECOMES ALLIES' GENERALISSIMO

On 26 March Marshal Ferdinand Foch became the de facto Supreme Allied Commander on the Western Front and on his shoulders fell the immediate problem of co-ordinating the defences and staunching the potentially fatal haemorrhage. Foch quickly realized that Amiens would be a key German target and must be defended at all costs. He was helped by Ludendorff, who opted to advance on too wide a front instead of focusing his efforts on taking Amiens. With every day the Allied line was becoming better reinforced and stronger, while the German line was becoming overstretched and weaker. The advance petered out on 8 April.

Ludendorff tried to regain the lost momentum by switching the point of attack. A fresh offensive was launched to the north, around the River Lys. Attacking here had been considered as an alternative to Operation Michael; it now became the focal point of a secondary onslaught. Again there was an immediate breakthrough which offered the Germans encouragement. On 11 April Haig issued a Special Order of the Day, a rallying call to all the ranks. 'There is no other course open to us but to fight it out. Every position must be held to the last man; there must be no retirement.' Originally he ended his stirring appeal to his hard-

pressed men with the words 'But be of good cheer, the British Empire must win in the end', but thought better of this optimistic note and struck it through.

By the end of April the new German offensive had again fizzled out. Ludendorff was in a cleft stick, caught between the need to make a decisive breakthrough and the need to conserve his dwindling resources. On 7 May Germany was buoyed by the news that Rumania had signed the Treaty of Bucharest and posed no further threat. After Russia's withdrawal Rumania had felt dangerously isolated and saw the need for an early armistice. Germany exacted a heavy price from the defeated country but it signified little. The war was now in its endgame phase and that had to be played out on the Western Front.

On 27 May Ludendorff tried yet another initiative, against the French Sixth Army along the Chemin des Dames. The German army swept across the Aisne and reached the Marne; Paris, only some 50 miles away, was threatened and a partial evacuation of the capital took place. The city did come under artillery fire but the attack was halted on the on the outskirts. In three months of concerted effort the German army had made great territorial

Below: Commemorating the Great War.

gains and inflicted considerable losses on the Allies, but as more and more American divisions poured into the theatre these were not as critical as the losses sustained by Ludendorff. In June alone the German army suffered over 200,000 casualties. That same month saw a further significant depletion in Ludendorff's manpower as a flu epidemic broke out among the ranks.

Ludendorff's final effort to achieve a breakthrough came on 15 July with an offensive around Reims. Three days later the French, supported by fresh American troops, countered. The Second Battle of the Marne, as it was called, was the turning point. From now until the end of hostilities Germany would be on the retreat. The Allies forced Ludendorff's army backwards relentlessly and the morale of the rival forces shifted accordingly, this time irrevocably.

On 8 August General Rawlinson led a combined Allied force in the Battle of Amiens, which caught the enemy off guard and quickly shattered any remaining hopes of victory. More than 2000 guns bombarded the German line and 400 tanks were deployed in support of the infantry. The recently formed RAF helped to give the Allies massive air supremacy. Also, the backroom staff had finally come up with their own solution to the problem of synchronizing machine-gun fire with the rotation of the propellers, something that Anthony Fokker had achieved for the Germans in 1915. Improvements in wireless telegraphy meant that reconnaissance aircraft could now relay information regarding enemy positions and batteries more efficiently. Although the attrition rate was high - on the first day of the Amiens offensive the RAF lost 45 planes to anti-aircraft fire — the contribution was significant.

'BLACK DAY' FOR GERMAN ARMY

The ferocity of the Amiens offensive prompted Ludendorff to declare it 'the black day of the German army'. The coup de grace would be to breach the Hindenburg Line — which finally came on 29 September — but even before that happened both Ludendorff and the Kaiser knew the outcome was now inevitable and the war had to be brought to an end.

Everywhere the noose around the Central Powers was tightening. On 27 September Bulgaria sued for peace, the first of Germany's allies to fall. There was widespread resentment among the Bulgarians that they had been treated as second-class citizens by the Reich,

not trusted allies. Scarce food resources were commandeered by the German army, leaving Bulgarian soldiers and civilians to go hungry. When the Allies launched a large-scale offensive from Salonika in mid-September Bulgaria's powers of resistance quickly ebbed away.

Defeat of the Ottoman Empire soon followed. Since taking Jerusalem in December 1917 General Allenby had been hampered by the redeployment of resources to the Western Front. In September 1918 he was ready to go on the attack once again. Allenby — 'the Bull' - expertly tricked his opposite number, Liman von Sanders, into thinking the point of attack would be inland. In fact Allenby struck along the coast, near Megiddo. The Turkish army, which had suffered heavily from guerrilla raids organized by the Arabs, assisted by T E Lawrence, was particularly weak in this area and a swift breakthrough was achieved. Damascus, Beirut and Aleppo fell in quick succession and Turkey finally capitulated on 30 October.

AUSTRIA — HUNGARY SUES FOR PEACE

Four days later Austria-Hungary submitted. The Dual Monarchy had been on the point of collapse for months, politically as well as militarily. Its disparate peoples had become increasingly unwilling to suffer further hardship for an empire to which they felt little allegiance. Following the Battle of the Piave in June 1918, in which the Austro-Hungarian army was rebuffed by the Italians, the commitment of the Hungarians, Croats, Czechs and Slavs was further eroded. Emperor Karl, the Imperial head of the Dual Monarchy since the death of Franz Joseph in November 1916, had already gone behind Germany's back in an attempt to secure a peace deal and save his country. Belatedly he offered autonomy to the main ethnic states over which he presided, but instead of binding the Austrian army together, the prospect of federal status served to further split the empire asunder. There was mass desertion as previously subject peoples sought to reach homelands which now had a new political identity. When the Italians launched their offensive on 24 October, Austrian resistance was virtually non-existent. On 3 November the Dual Monarchy accepted terms.

Even before Germany lost her chief ally the leadership knew it was time for the Reich to yield. On 4 October the new chancellor Prince Max of Baden

Left: Philippe Pétain, who was replaced as France's military commander by Foch in March 1918. Following the Allied victory he was created Marshal for his heroic efforts in the defence of his country. A generation later he would be vilified as head of the Vichy government which collaborated with the Nazis.

Meuse-Argonne region, which began on 26 September. The aim was to capture vital rail links that were Germany's main line of communication. Over the next five weeks the American army sustained over 100,000 casualties but on 1 November the final breakthrough of the war was achieved. Ludendorff had already fallen by then and it was only a matter of time before his country followed. On 3 November the German navy mutinied at Kiel and there was revolution on the streets of Berlin. On 8 November Marshal Foch received Germany's armistice delegation in a railway carriage in the forest of Compiegne. The defeated country was given seventy-two hours to agree to the terms laid down, which included

sent a note to Washington hoping to secure an armistice based on Wilson's Fourteen Points, which was considered to be the least worst option. If Germany expected more favourable terms from America than Britain or France she was to be disappointed. The Reich had no bargaining chips and would have to accept whatever terms were imposed, a fact not lost on the US president. Wilson didn't apprise the British or French of the dialogue entered into between Washington and Berlin, exchanges which reached a conclusion with Germany's acceptance of US terms on 27 October.

Meanwhile Foch continued to turn the screw. General Pershing's American forces, supported by the French, were at the forefront of a huge offensive in the

democratization. The German delegation didn't need three days to deliberate. The following day the Kaiser abdicated, decamping to neutral Holland. The armistice was signed at 5.00am on 11 November, to come into force six hours later. Some German soldiers fought to the last minute before laying down their weapons. While Foch acclaimed the Allied victory as 'the greatest battle in history', von Hindenburg led his defeated troops home to a country in chaos. All the privation and hardship had failed to produce a glorious victory and mobs vented their anger by attacking the war-weary officers of the Reich.

The war had been won. It now fell to the victors to shape a peace in which principles and ideals would clash with self-interest.

Right: January 1918. A group of
soldiers huddles around a fire as
the war enters yet another year.
The outcome still lay in the
balance. With Russia suing for
peace the Central Powers had
finally achieved their goal of
having to fight on just one
major front.

Below: A new year but the same
terrain. Events in 1918, far
from becoming bogged down,
were to move very quickly.

Above: Fresh troops disembark in France, a daily scene at the country's ports. During 1918 American troops would also pour into the country to bolster the Entente Powers' war effort.

Wilson's 14 Points

On 8 January 1918 President Woodrow Wilson delivered his famous '14 Points' speech to Congress. These embodied his vision for an immediate peace settlement and for future security. They included arms reduction and the lifting of trade barriers. Self-determination was a theme which ran throughout. Austria and Hungary should be divided into separate nations; Poland, the Balkan states and peoples of the Ottoman Empire should have their autonomy and sovereignty guaranteed. Wilson's final point outlined the establishment of an international association of states, a forum for nations to air grievances and for conflict resolution. This would be constituted as the League of Nations a year later, although the hopes invested in it were to be dashed in the light of the experience of the interwar years.

Right: 26 March 1918, five days after the launch of Ludendorff's audacious plan to gain victory before US forces arrived in numbers. The aim of the 'Kaisers Battle' was to divide the enemy. The British army was to be pushed back to the Channel, after which it was thought the French would collapse.

Below: Highland troops marching to meet Germany's new grand offensive. The initial gains were spectacular: the German army rapidly advanced 14 miles, the greatest movement since the opposing forces became entrenched in the autumn of 1914.

Treaty of Brest-Litovsk

On 3 March 1918 the Treaty of Brest-Litovsk, concluded between Germany and Russia, formally ended the latter's involvement in the war. Russia paid a heavy price for an end to hostilities, ceding vast tracts of land and a sizable portion of her resources. It was almost a year to the day since the Tsar's abdication, for most of which time he and his family had been held comfortably, but under guard, in the Siberian town of Tobolsk.

Above: 3 April 1918. British army on the back foot. The allied response to the German onslaught was not helped by divisions and mistrust between Haig and Pétain. The latter offered little support at the time when the British army was already under strength.

Germany's spring offensive

Going into 1918 the balance of power remained
delicately poised. The elimination of the Russian
threat was a major boost to Germany, and a year of
unrestricted submarine warfare had had significant
results. On the other hand the allied naval blockade
was also biting. Germany's domestic economy was in a
parlous state, the civilian population subject to the
kind of privation which was only supportable in the
short term. The coming year would also see American
troops arrive on the battlefront, making a protracted
war even riskier.   Ludendorff's answer to all these
issues was a large-scale spring offensive. In a departure
from previous thinking – when France had been
targeted as the weaker of the Entente Powers on the
Western front – this time Ludendorff decided to
strike at the British army.

Above: A French village
alive with troop
movement, 2 April
1918. Few Americans
had as yet reached the
combat zone, despite
the fact that a year had
elapsed since the
country had declared
war.

Left: An officer looks on as an ammunition dump is exploded prior to a tactical withdrawal. The German army's tactic of short, ferocious artillery bombardments followed by an advance of elite storm troopers initially proved highly successful against the depleted and exhausted British ranks.

Below: Soldiers temporarily relieved of frontline duty. March 1918 had seen British troops on the retreat. In April the German juggernaut was halted.

The 'Kaiser's battle'

Ludendorff devised a bold plan to bring the war to a swift conclusion before the domestic economy collapsed and the will of the people was crushed. The intention was to drive a wedge between the British and French armies, pushing the former back to the Channel coast. The 'Kaiser's battle' was launched on 21 March 1918. Russia's withdrawal from the war allowed Ludendorff to redeploy men to the area between Arras and St Quentin, where the focal point of the attack would be. 7000 guns unleashed one million shells. General Sir Hubert Gough's Fifth Army bore the brunt as the German forces, with storm troops in the vanguard, made spectacular gains. By July the map of the Western front had been radically altered as Germany advanced more than 20 miles in places. But it was a bulge, not a breakthrough. The attacking army was over-extended and exhausted when the allies launched their massive counter-offensive on 18 July, 1918.

Above: 28 March 1918. Field guns on the battlefield at Arras. This was a turning point in the bold German offensive as British forces stemmed the advancing tide.

Above: A battery of 60-pounders in action at Arras. Ludendorff had been a victim of his own success. The storm troopers had advanced beyond the range of supporting artillery, making them vulnerable to a counterstrike.

The greatest battle of all

This morning the enemy renewed his attacks in great strength along practically the whole battle front. Fierce fighting has taken place in our battle positions and is still continuing.

From reports received from all parts of the battle front the enemy has made some progress at certain points. At others his troops have been thrown back by our counter-attacks. Our losses have inevitably been considerable, but not out of proportion to the magnitude of the battle.

From reports received from all parts of the battle front the enemy's losses continue to be very heavy, and his advance has everywhere been made at a great sacrifice. Our troops are fighting with the greatest gallantry. When all ranks and all units of every arm have behaved so well it is difficult at this stage of the battle to distinguish instances.

From SIR DOUGLAS HAIG.
Daily Mail, 23 March 1918

Above: 9 April 1918. These British troops would not have realized it but the crisis point had just passed. Four days earlier the German army had failed to take Amiens; the 'Kaiser's battle' had finally stalled.

The line holds, but the crises is not past

The British Army has made its valiant answer to Sir Douglas Haig's general order calling upon it to stand and fight – to the last man – for 'the safety of our homes and the freedom of mankind'. For the past forty-eight hours, in the face of repeated attacks by masses of Germans and of a terrific bombardment, our devoted lads have held their ground firmly and unflinchingly. The line is still unbroken, and though the crisis is not yet by any means over, there is at least good hope that the men of 1918 will hold fast and win through like the heroes of 1914.

Daily Mail, 14 April 1918

Above: The German advance in late March, early April had yielded remarkable territorial gains. Both sides now realized that control of extra ground without a breakthrough was actually worth very little.

Right: A sign indicates the dividing line between the British and Belgian sectors. An increasingly desperate Ludendorff switched the point of attack to Flanders after failing in Picardy.

Below: 3 May 1918. A British division pictured after an inspection by France's premier, Georges Clemenceau. With every passing day the Entente powers were being strengthened by American troops. The German army, by contrast, had been seriously depleted by Ludendorff's failed gamble.

Above: Street fighting in Bailleul.
Household goods and chattels
provide an effective barricade for
these soldiers.

Above: British troops and marching companions at Verneuil, 29 May 1918. The spring brought further good news for the allies as Germany's thrust in Italy was halted. Ludendorff was unable to spare resources to exploit the impressive gains made following the Battle of Caporetto.

Left: Men of the 4th Battalion, 29th Division in optimistic mood as they march to the front in Achxeux, June 1918. At the beginning of the month the German army reached the Marne, as they had done in September 1914. Once again they were halted, tantalizingly short of the French capital.

The Royal Air Force

Today the Royal Air Force comes into being. The Royal Flying Corps and the Royal Naval Air Service are amalgamated under one control. The interests of both are served by the Air Ministry with a single thought to the efficiency of the whole. The results of this merging of two forces will be seen chiefly in unity of effort and economy of material. Competition for the services of men and in the use of material will disappear. Construction of machines will proceed more rapidly, and the feeling that one branch of the service is receiving more attention than the other will disappear. There will be one uniform for the Air Force, ingeniously combining the characteristics of each branch.

Daily Mail, 1 April 1918

Above: Roll-call in a labour camp. The names of these Chinese are inscribed on streamers attached to a rotating drum.

Above: A company of British soldiers in place to defend a canal in France, 22 May 1918. Having failed to achieve a breakthrough against the British, Ludendorff targeted the French front line but once again with only partial success.

Right: A British soldier tries to protect himself from shrapnel as shells explode nearby.

June 1918. A British intelligence sergeant examines a civilian's papers. Many German soldiers on leave never returned to active duty as morale among both civilians and military personnel plummeted. The majority of the German people – those who could not afford to pay black market prices – had had enough of living on the breadline. German soldiers in increasing numbers began to see the war as a lost cause and a pointless sacrifice.

'Black day of the German army'

In mid-July 1918 the German army had the French capital within its sights, just as it had in August 1914. In the Second Battle of the Marne the allies again ensured that the enemy got no nearer to Paris. From this point on Germany would be on the retreat; the will of the army and civilian population to continue the struggle would be eroded with every passing day. On 8 August an allied attack around the Somme, spearheaded by 450 tanks, was more than a comprehensive victory; it also saw demoralized German troops surrendering in numbers. Fresh soldiers brought up to staunch the flow attracted scornful cries of 'black leg' from their dispirited comrades, their actions seen as simply prolonging the misery. Ludendorff described it as 'the black day of the German army' and realized that the outcome of the war was no longer in doubt.

Above: British engineers camouflaging a barbed wire trap, July 1918. Ludendorff was contemplating a fresh attack this month when the allies wrested the initiative by going on the attack.

Left: Cavalry passing the ruins of Albert Cathedral. The Allied counter-offensive was measured rather than bold. Limited objectives supported by an accurate creeping barrage proved highly effective. The German army would now be in retreat until the signing of the Armistice.

Left: French engineers sweeping the street in Noyon for mines. The German army attempted a breakthrough in Noyon in June 1918 and Reims the following month. Neither proved successful. Mine-laying prior to withdrawal was a common practice.

Sweeping gains

Scenes of attritional warfare and minimal movement were over by the summer of 1918. The successes the German army had enjoyed in the spring alarmed the British government, which responded by authorizing a significant deployment of fresh troops. Ludendorff also massively underestimated the strength of the American Expeditionary Force and the impact it would make. On 8 August 1918 an allied attack near the Somme, supported by over 400 tanks, brought sweeping gains. Ludendorff described this as a 'black day of the German army' as soldiers surrendered in droves.

Decisive gains

In August and September 1918 the Allies made gains at a dizzying speed compared to the long years in which there had been hardly any movement. Albert, Bapaume, Peronne and Noyon all fell. Allied troops swept across the battlefields of the Somme in a matter of days. On 12 September General Pershing led the first all-American offensive, successfully taking the St. Miheil salient. By the end of the month the Hindenburg Line was finally breached.

Above: Australian troops prepare to go over the top at Mont St Quentin, 2 September 1918. This was part of a concerted attack devised by the generalissimo of the Entente Powers, Marshal Foch. The aim was to rupture the Hindenburg Line, which would bring victory within the allies' grasp.

Above: Keeping watch through a camouflaged periscope. German resistance was ebbing away at an alarming rate. To make matters worse for Ludendorff an influenza epidemic broke out. Over the next year this would claim far more lives than the war itself. The immediate problem for Ludendorff was the fact that thousands of his troops were laid low just as the entente powers were stretching his resources to the limit.

One million US troops

By September one million US troops had arrived in France. Initially the Americans wished to remain as an independent force under the command of General John Pershing. It was later agreed that Pershing's men would be deployed by Foch where and when he deemed necessary. Pershing himself led a U.S. force which played a vital role in the attack on the Meuse Valley, launched 26 September. This offensive was the final squeeze which convinced Germany's military leaders that defeat was inevitable.

Above: 6 September 1918.
The ridge of North Peronne
ablaze in the wake of the
German army's retreat.

Right: Peronne Cathedral had
been reduced to a shell when
the allies entered the town
on 18 September 1918. In
less than a week the Allies
gained more ground in the
Somme region than in six
months' fighting in the
bloodbath of 1916.

Above: On patrol in Albert, which had been captured by the allies on 23 August 1918.

Left: British soldiers on the outskirts of Thiepval, 5 September 1918. As the allies continued to exert a stranglehold the Kaiser made representations that Germany was prepared to settle. Germany was in no position to bargain and the allies were certainly in no mood to deal with the Kaiser. Military defeat and political change would go in tandem.

Above: 14 September
1918. Australian
troops warily pass a
possible booby trap as
they pursue the
retreating German
army in the Somme
region.

Right: Firing from the
cover of a half-
destroyed war in
Albert. In the last
days of September
the Hindenburg Line
was finally breached.
In the following week
Allied forces smashed
it across its entire
length.

Above: A lone soldier in Peronne Square, shortly after the German army's withdrawal. There were no reinforcements for Ludendorff to call upon. He would blame the lack of civilian support for the military failure, a crude ploy to exonerate himself from blame.

Germany looks for peace

One of many French towns which bore the scars of occupation but were now liberated. On 29 September Bulgaria signed an armistice, the first of the Central powers to do so. Ludendorff wanted Germany to do the same. He and other senior figures realized that the enemy would be more inclined to deal with a Germany reconstituted as a parliamentary democracy untainted by the events of the past four years. On 3 October Prince Max of Baden was appointed Chancellor. He immediately sued for a peace settlement along the lines of Woodrow Wilson's 14 points.

Above: 5 October 1918.
Advancing in Cambrai. While the
political machinations were taking
place, the allied troops advanced
relentlessly. The loyal rump of
the German army continued to
fight a rearguard action against
overwhelming odds.

Opposite: Canadian troops in Cambrai,
which fell on 8 October 1918. By
then the allies had rejected Germany's
offer of peace. Ludendorff had
correctly anticipated that with every
passing day Germany's hand was
weaker and the Entente Powers had
no reason to settle.

Allied troops take control in France. Removing the German army from French soil was one of the few long-cherished objectives of the war. The collapse of the German army had come so swiftly that the allies had given little thought to what each wanted from the peace settlement.

Above: Buildings in Cambrai
reduced to burnt-out shells.
Meanwhile, the German war
machine continued to crumble.
Ludendorff resigned on 27
October. Three days later
Turkey signed an armistice,
followed by Austria-Hungary
on 3 November.

Opposite: Allied troops climbing the banks of the
St Quentin canal, 23 October 1918. By now they
were virtually unopposed. In a last throw of the
dice the German navy was ordered to put to sea.
The sailors had endured intolerable conditions
and were not prepared to risk sacrifice in a
hopeless venture. There was mutiny at Kiel and
Wilhelmshaven, and in many cases the ships'
engines were sabotaged by their crew.

Right: Cheers of victory. The Allied soldiers had done their work, though at a high cost. Some 4.5 million had died for the cause. The death toll for the Central Powers was in the region of 4 million, although the exact figure is not known.

Below: 9 December 1918. The signpost denotes that these cavalrymen are entering German territory. That territory would be considerably depleted in the peace settlement, although Germany was not fragmented in the way that the Austro-Hungarian and Ottoman empires were.

Armistice signed

In early October Germany's new Chancellor, Prince Max of Baden, sought peace terms along the lines of Woodrow Wilson's 14 points. The allies were in no mood to settle, and certainly not on terms of Germany's choosing. The armistice was signed at 5:00a.m. on 11 November 1918, to come into force six hours later. At 11:00a.m. on the 11th day of the 11th month, the Great War officially came to an end.

Above: 23 November 1918. The opening of the first military bridge, across the Scheldt at Tournai.

General Election held

Soldiers queuing to register their vote in the general election, held on 14 December 1918. Unsurprisingly, Lloyd George was returned to office, having led the country to victory. The political situation in Germany was far more volatile. On 9 November Prince Max of Baden handed over the Chancellorship to moderate Socialist Friedrich Ebert. On the same day Kaiser Wilhelm II was informed that his abdication was necessary for the political stability of the country. Germany, like Russia a year earlier, was on the verge of revolution. The country had its own Bolshevik agitators in Rosa Luxemburg and Karl Liebnecht, who headed the Spartacist League. On 10 November the Weimar Republic was born. Ebert immediately sought an understanding with the military, whose compliance was essential if revolution was to be avoided. He received that assurance. Luxemburg and Liebnecht were both murdered early in 1919.

The lucky families were reunited and could at least attempt to put the events of the past four years behind them. Politically, there was no going back; a peace shaped by a demand for retribution and restorative justice ensured that post-conflict Europe would be dogged by bitterness and resentment.

CHAPTER SIX

An Uneasy Peace

Prosecuting a war in which some 10 million people had lost their lives had been such an all-encompassing undertaking that the Allies had given little thought to the peace terms they would exact. The only coherent document in place was Woodrow Wilson's Fourteen Points, and the idealism enshrined in these had a natural and wide-ranging appeal. Instead of disparate peoples subsumed within great imperial structures there would be new states, whose citizens would have a common language and culture. There would be an arms reduction programme, and a new League of Nations would oversee conflict resolution. Peace, prosperity and security for all was a seductive message to a continent that had been ravaged by war for over four years.

The end of hostilities saw the collapse of three mighty empires. In Russia the Romanovs had already lost power, and on 17 July 1918 Tsar Nicholas II and his family were executed in Ekaterinburg. Now the Austro-Hungarian and Ottoman empires were also dismembered. The Hohenzollerns, who had ruled Prussia since 1701 and provided Germany with her imperial leader since 1871, also disappeared from the political map, although the country itself remained as an entity. But Wilson's grand design for what should replace these monolithic structures was fraught with difficulty. Redrawing Europe into smaller nation states along homogeneous lines was an impossible task, and the misconceived attempt merely stored up trouble for the future.

The idealism of the Wilsonian vision was not given a free rein. Lloyd George and France's premier, George Clemenceau, had a different agenda. There was a demand not simply for a just peace but for punitive measures. France in particular wanted to ensure that her Teutonic neighbour's bellicose ways were at an end, and not just temporarily. There was also the question of the division of hard-won spoils, including dividends to Romania and Italy, whose support had been secured with promises that they would profit from victory.

LEAGUE OF NATIONS ESTABLISHED
At the Paris Peace Conference, which opened on 18 January 1919, Wilson laid down the articles of the League of Nations Covenant before the assembled delegates. Almost from the outset the new body was emasculated. Even the US Congress refused to ratify the Covenant, wary of the involvement in distant quarrels that it implied. Even so, by the end of 1919 the Covenant had been incorporated into the various peace treaties and membership of the new League extended far beyond countries which had participated in the war. In the longer term its effectiveness was severely compromised. The inter-war years revealed that it was a toothless tiger. It became clear that the League lacked the will to impose sanctions and if necessary back them up with force. It was eventually wound up in 1945.

Five separate peace treaties were signed between the Allies and each of the defeated powers. The first of those, the settlement with Germany, was the most significant. The Treaty of Versailles was signed in the palace's Hall of Mirrors on 28 June 1919. The terms imposed were severe: Alsace-Lorraine was returned to France; most of East Prussia was lost to the reconstituted Poland, which was also given access to the sea via Danzig; the Saar region was to be administered by the League of Nations, and there would be a 15-year Allied occupation of the Rhineland; Germany's colonies were forfeit; Belgium and Denmark gained territory at Germany's expense; she was not allowed to maintain either a U-boat fleet or air force, while her army was not to exceed 100,000; the High Seas Fleet was interned at Scapa Flow.

Below: A bugler sounds the fall-in to a company billeted in an Austrian village, 12 February, 1919. The following day Woodrow Wilson presented the Covenant for the League of Nations, which it was hoped would settle international disputes and obviate the need for countries to resort to armed aggression. The Allies adopted the Covenant, albeit with reservations. Wilson failed to get it through a Congress which was still isolationist by inclination.

Opposite: The road to recovery. Local trade being revived in the devastated mining town of Lens, August 1919. The punitive reparations imposed on Germany for damage of this kind were unsustainable. Many on the victors' side believed the price exacted was too great. Among them was the economist John Maynard Keynes, a member of the British delegation at Versailles, who resigned in protest.

Two further stipulations were controversial and would have counter-productive ramifications. The first concerned the question of reparations. Clemenceau led the demand for Germany to suffer a heavy financial penalty, just as France herself had been made to pay following the Franco-Prussian War of 1870-71. The US did not ratify the treaty and waived all claims to reparations, leaving France and Britain to settle the issue. Lloyd George and Clemenceau imposed an interim order for Germany to pay $5 billion in cash and goods, with the issue to be re-examined at a future date. Set at such a level, the reparations were cripplingly punitive and within four years Germany had defaulted. By the end of the 1920s it was clear that the payments were unsustainable and they were allowed to lapse. Economic hardship and the bitter resentment

it fostered would provide fertile ground for Adolf Hitler's National Socialist Party, established in 1921.

In addition to their financial demands the Allies also insisted on adding a moral dimension to the peace settlement. A clause was included asserting Germany's moral culpability for the conflict. Germany contested that she bore sole responsibility and even garnered support among her former enemies on this point. The Kaiser and other high-ranking Germans were set to face trial for war crimes, although in the event this was not carried out. The sympathies engendered by what was seen as blatant vindictiveness allowed appeasement towards Germany to take hold during much of the inter-war period.

BIRTH OF YUGOSLAVIA

The Treaty of Saint-Germain, signed 10 September 1919, created a new Republic of Austria, with Italy gaining some of her former territory. The independence of Czechoslovakia, Poland and Hungary was recognized. The break-up of the Austro-Hungarian empire also allowed Serbia's pre-war wish for a Slav state to be accommodated. The Kingdom of Serbs, Croats and Slovenes – later renamed Yugoslavia – was born, with Alexander I as its first head of state. This new country also included Bosnians, Macedonians and Albanians, an ethnic mix that would create tensions and, seventy years later, lead to internecine war.

Settlement with Bulgaria came with the Treaty of Neuilly, signed 27 November 1919. Under its terms Bulgaria ceded land to Greece, Romania and Yugoslavia, including its outlet to the Aegean Sea. Hungary was reduced to a fraction of its former size by the Treaty of Trianon, signed 4 June 1920. Romania got Transylvania, the price for which she had gone to war, while Czechoslovakia and Yugoslavia also profited territorially.

The final agreement, the Treaty of Sevres, was signed with Turkey on 10 August 1920. Mesopotamia and Palestine both became British mandates, while Syria became a French mandate. Turkey also lost territory to Greece and Italy. This treaty quickly unravelled. A nationalist movement led by Mustafa Kemal resented the conciliatory approach adopted by Sultan Mehmed VI. Kemal swept to power on a promise of recovering some of the country's lost territory. On 24 July 1923, following a bitter struggle against Greece, the Treaty of Lausanne was signed.

Under its terms Turkey regained Thrace and Smyrna, which had been given to Greece under the imposed settlement three years earlier.

The peace treaties caused much ill feeling, and not only by those countries which had experienced territorial and financial losses. Italy thought she should have gained a greater share of the victors' spoils. In 1919 Benito Mussolini formed a new political party, Fasci di Combattimento, whose chief aim was to restore Italy's national pride. One method of achieving this was by acquisition, and under Il Duce's dictatorial rule Italy looked to Africa to exert its influence.

PEACE TREATIES FOSTER RESENTMENT

Far from being settled and peaceful, post-conflict Europe was beset by economic hardship and border disputes. The continent's redrawn map left all of the newly formed states with disaffected minorities. But Germany remained the greatest problem. The country had been deeply wounded but not dismembered in the way the Austro-Hungarian and Ottoman empires had. The peace terms were punitive enough to provoke an acrimonious response but, as events would show, Germany was not permanently shackled in the way that France had wanted. Germany herself was admitted to the League of Nations in 1926, but when Adolf Hitler assumed power seven years later one of his earliest acts was to withdraw from that body. Shortly afterwards he repudiated the military constraints imposed by the Treaty of Versailles and Germany embarked on a massive rearmament programme.

The perceived vindictiveness of the 1919 treaty would come to be seen as instrumental in Hitler's rise to power and the events which followed. In 1919 some prescient voices were already warning that war had not been concluded, merely suspended. Far from being 'a war to end all wars', the 1914-18 conflict would eventually be regarded as a prelude to World War Two.

Opposite: Veterans of the Ypres campaigns march past the town's famous Cloth Hall, 21 May 1920. Strict limits were imposed on Germany's military strength: her standing army was not to exceed 100,000, and there was to be no submarine fleet or air force. Many career soldiers – including Adolf Hitler – channelled their efforts into the political domain instead. Shortly after becoming Chancellor in 1933, Hitler renounced the treaty obligations regarding Germany's military capability and launched a programme of rearmament.

Post-war peace talks

British and French leaders, pictured during the postwar peace talks. Clemenceau (second left) did not embrace the new world order espoused by Woodrow Wilson. He wanted a Europe along prewar lines, but with France holding the balance of power. Like Clemenceau, Lloyd George (third left) believed that Germany bore full responsibility for starting the war, which was enshrined in the controversial Article 231. However, he also saw a prosperous Germany as important to the future stability of the continent, which in turn was vital to the protection of Britain's worldwide interests. The flaws in the Treaty of Versailles were highlighted almost immediately. It satisfied virtually no one, solved virtually nothing. It did set the political agenda for the rest of the twentieth century, including sowing the seeds for an even costlier conflict barely twenty years later.

THE WAR IN BRIEF

1914

AUG. 4.
Britain at war with Germany.

AUG. 20.
Brussels occupied.

AUG. 23.
Mons Battle.

AUG. 26.
Russians defeated at
Tannenberg.

SEPT. 6.
Battle at Marne; Paris saved.

OCT. 9.
Antwerp occupied.

OCT. 11.
Battle of Ypres;
Channel ports saved.

DEC. 8.
Naval battle off Falklands.

DEC. 14.
Shelling of Scarborough.

1915

JAN. 24.
Naval battle off Dogger Bank.

APRIL 25.
Allies land in Gallipoli.

MAY 2.
Russian front broken.

MAY 7.
Lusitania torpedoed.

MAY 23.
Italy declared war.

AUG. 4.
Fall of Warsaw.

SEPT. 25.
Battle of Loos.

OCT. 13.
Murder of Nurse Cavell.

NOV. 22.
Turks routed at Ctesiphon.

1916

JAN. 8.
Evacuation of Gallipoli.

APRIL 29.
Surrender of Kut.

MAY 31.
Naval battle off Jutland.

JULY 1.
British attack on the Somme.

AUG. 6.
Battle of the Isonzo.

DEC. 6.
Fall of Bucharest

DEC. 15.
German failure at Verdun.

1917

FEB. 1.
Unrestricted U-boat blockade.

MARCH 11.
Fall of Baghdad.

MARCH 12.
Revolution in Russia.

APRIL 5.
United States declared war.

APRIL 9.
Battle of Arras.

OCT. 24.
Italian retreat from Caporetto

DEC. 9.
Fall of Jerusalem.

1918

FEB. 10.
Russia out of the war.

MARCH 21.
Great German offensive begun.

APRIL 22.
Naval raid on Zeebrugge and
Ostend.

JULY 18.
Turn of the tide.

SEPT. 30.
Bulgaria surrenders. Fall of
Damascus.

OCT. 1.
St. Quentin retaken.

OCT. 17.
Ostend, Lille and Douai
recaptured.

OCT. 26 .
Fall of Aleppo.

OCT. 30.
Turkey surrenders.

NOV. 8
Austria surrenders.

NOV. 11.
Capture of Mons,
Germany surrenders.

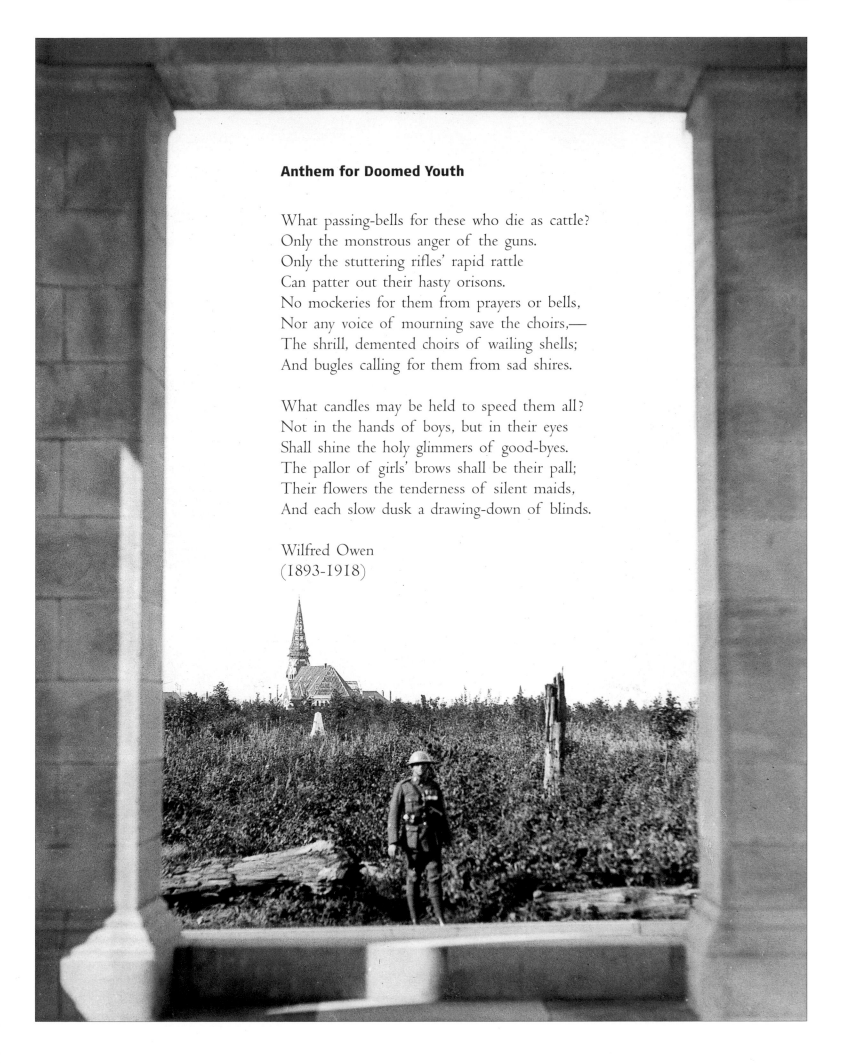

Anthem for Doomed Youth

What passing-bells for these who die as cattle?
Only the monstrous anger of the guns.
Only the stuttering rifles' rapid rattle
Can patter out their hasty orisons.
No mockeries for them from prayers or bells,
Nor any voice of mourning save the choirs,—
The shrill, demented choirs of wailing shells;
And bugles calling for them from sad shires.

What candles may be held to speed them all?
Not in the hands of boys, but in their eyes
Shall shine the holy glimmers of good-byes.
The pallor of girls' brows shall be their pall;
Their flowers the tenderness of silent maids,
And each slow dusk a drawing-down of blinds.

Wilfred Owen
(1893-1918)